Qualitative Methods for Institutional Research

Eileen Kuhns, S. V. Martorana, *Editors*

NEW DIRECTIONS FOR INSTITUTIONAL RESEARCH
Sponsored by the Association for Institutional Research
MARVIN W. PETERSON, *Editor-in-Chief*

Number 34, June 1982

Paperback sourcebooks in
The Jossey-Bass Higher Education Series

Jossey-Bass Inc., Publishers
San Francisco • Washington • London

Qualitative Methods for Institutional Research
Volume IX, Number 2, June 1982
Eileen Kuhns, S. V. Martorana, *Editors*

New Directions for Institutional Research Series
Marvin W. Peterson, *Editor-in-Chief*

New Directions for Institutional Research (publication number
USPS 098-830) is published quarterly by Jossey-Bass Inc.,
Publishers, and is sponsored by the Association for Institutional
Research. The volume and issue numbers above are included for
the convenience of libraries. Second-class postage rates paid at
San Francisco, California, and at additional mailing offices.

Correspondence:
Subscriptions, single-issue orders, change of address notices,
undelivered copies, and other correspondence should be sent to
New Directions Subscriptions, Jossey-Bass Inc., Publishers,
433 California Street, San Francisco, California 94104.

Editorial correspondence should be sent to the Editor-in-Chief,
Marvin W. Peterson, Center for the Study of Higher Education,
University of Michigan, Ann Arbor, Michigan 48109.

Library of Congress Catalogue Card Number LC 81-48574
International Standard Serial Number ISSN 0271-0579
International Standard Book Number ISBN 87589-904-8

Cover art by Willi Baum
Manufactured in the United States of America

Ordering Information

The paperback sourcebooks listed below are published quarterly and can be ordered either by subscription or as single copies.

Subscriptions cost $35.00 per year for institutions, agencies, and libraries. Individuals can subscribe at the special rate of $21.00 per year *if payment is by personal check.* (Note that the full rate of $35.00 applies if payment is by institutional check, even if the subscription is designated for an individual.) Standing orders are accepted.

Single copies are available at $7.95 when payment accompanies order, and *all single-copy orders under $25.00 must include payment.* (California, Washington, D.C., New Jersey, and New York residents please include appropriate sales tax.) For billed orders, cost per copy is $7.95 plus postage and handling. (Prices subject to change without notice.)

To ensure correct and prompt delivery, all orders must give either the *name of an individual* or an *official purchase order number.* Please submit your order as follows:

Subscriptions: specify series and subscription year.
Single Copies: specify sourcebook code and issue number (such as, IR8).

Mail orders for United States and Possessions, Latin America, Canada, Japan, Australia, and New Zealand to:
Jossey-Bass Inc., Publishers
433 California Street
San Francisco, California 94104

Mail orders for all other parts of the world to:
Jossey-Bass Limited
28 Banner Street
London EC1Y 8QE

New Directions for Institutional Research Series
Marvin W. Peterson, *Editor-in-Chief*

Contents

Editors' Notes

This volume of *New Directions for Institutional Research* focuses on the potential of qualitative methodology for institutional planning, policy formulation, and decision making. The dominance of the quantitative paradigm in current institutional research is reflected in the titles of papers presented at the annual AIR forums and the recent monograph, *The Functions of Institutional Research* (Saupe, 1981), sponsored by the publications board of the Association for Institutional Research (AIR).

Neither the coeditors nor the authors of chapters in this volume take the position that either the quantitative or the qualitative research paradigm is superior. Instead, the two paradigms are viewed as complementary, each adding a needed dimension to information that supports planning, policy development, and decision making in postsecondary institutions.

This volume goes beyond discussion of the substantive difference between qualitative and quantitative measurement, design, and analysis. It examines qualitative research applications in key functional areas of institutional operations, and it discusses the combination of qualitative and quantitative methods in a mixed model that does not confuse the two methods or sacrifice their particular strengths.

A definitional chapter by Michael Quinn Patton opens the volume. It is followed by four chapters illustrating theoretical approaches to qualitative methodology of anthropology and sociology, mathematics, political science and public administration, and history. The next four chapters feature applications of qualitative methodology, in decisions about students, in academic decisions, in management and finance decisions, and in decisions for strengthening educational practice. The volume concludes with a chapter by George W. Bonham on the choice of quality measurements as a basis for institutional and public action and a summary chapter by coeditors S. V. Martorana and Eileen Kuhns.

Eileen Kuhns
S. V. Martorana
Editors

1

2

Reference

Saupe, J. L. *The Functions of Institutional Research.* Tallahassee, Fla.: Association for Institutional Research, 1981.

Eileen Kuhns is an associate professor and coordinator of the Education Administration Program, Catholic University of America.

S. V. Martorana is a professor in the College of Education and a research associate in the Center for the Study of Higher Education, Pennsylvania State University. They are codirectors of a FIPSE-funded project designed to institutionalize an interorganizational, interstate program of regionwide planning for postsecondary education.

The evidence is that we are running most of the
time on preprogrammed tapes. That has always
been the function of scientific paradigms.

Qualitative Methods
and Approaches:
What Are They?

Michael Quinn Patton

In carrying out an institutional analysis, a variety of methods and
measurement decisions must typically be made. What to study?
How to study it? How long to conduct the study? How to assure
that data are valid, reliable, and useful? How to analyse the data?
What conclusions to draw? Answers to these basic questions
involve trade-offs and choices among a complex array of alternatives as we attempt to be responsive and adaptable to the research
situation in which we find ourselves. But, how do we actually
behave when faced with such complex decisions and choices? The
evidence from social and behavioral science is that, in other areas of
decision making, when faced with complex choices and multiple
possibilities, we fall back on a set of rules and standard operating
procedures that predetermines what we will do, effectively short-
circuits our situational adaptability. The evidence is that we are
running most of the time on preprogrammed tapes. That has
always been the function of scientific paradigms. Faced with a new
situation, the scientist unconsciously turns to paradigmatic rules

E. Kuhns, S. V. Martorana (Eds.). *New Directions for Institutional Research: Qualitative
Methods for Institutional Research*, no. 34. San Francisco: Jossey-Bass, March 1982.

to find out what to do. This may help to explain why so many researchers who have genuinely embraced the ideology of situational problem solving in research find that the approaches in which they have been trained and with which they are most comfortable just happen to be particularly appropriate in every new research situation that they confront, time after time after time. (For an elaboration of the problems of situational flexibility in research designs, see Patton, 1981.)

A paradigm is a world view, a general perspective, a way of breaking down the complexity of the real world. As such, paradigms are deeply embedded in the socialization of adherents and practitioners. Paradigms tell them what is important, legitimate, and reasonable. Paradigms are also normative, telling the practitioner what to do, eliminating the need for long existential or epistemological consideration. This aspect of paradigms constitutes both their strength and their weakness—their strength in that it makes action possible, their weakness in that the reason for action is hidden in the unquestioned assumptions of the paradigm.

Paradigms make it possible for researchers to engage in normal science, the work of filling in the details and testing the individual hypotheses of major theories. There is not a lot of room for situational adaptability in Kuhn's (1970) description of normal science: "Scientists work from models acquired through education and through subsequent exposure to the literature, often without quite knowing or needing to know what characteristics have given these models the status of community paradigms. . . . That scientists do not usually ask or debate what makes a particular problem or solution legitimate tempts us to suppose that, at least intuitively, they know the answer. But, it may only indicate that neither the question nor the answer is felt to be relevant to their research. Paradigms may be prior to, more binding, and more complete than any set of rules for research that could be unequivocally abstracted from them" (Kuhn, 1970, p. 46).

Social and behavioral science has been denominated by the natural science paradigm of hypothetico-deductive methodology. This dominant paradigm assumes quantitative measurement, experimental design, and multivariate, parametric statistical analysis to be the epitome of good science. The basic model for conducting institutional research under this paradigm comes from the tradition of experimentation in agriculture, which gave us many of the basic statistical and experimental techniques widely used in social science research.

By way of contrast, the alternative to the dominant hypothetico-deductive paradigm is derived from the tradition of anthropological field studies. Using the techniques of in-depth, open-ended interviewing and personal observation, the alternative paradigm relies on qualitative data, holistic analysis, and detailed description derived from close contact with the targets of study. The hypothetico-deductive, natural science paradigm aims at prediction of social phenomena; the holistic-inductive, anthropological paradigm aims at understanding of social phenomena.

Neither of these paradigms is intrinsically better than the other for institutional research. Instead, they represent alternatives between which institutional researchers can choose. Moreover, there are a number of ways in which both qualitative and quantitative approaches can be combined or used simultaneously. Thus, we want to avoid posing the problem as one of the dominant paradigm versus the alternative paradigm, of experimental designs based on quantitative measurement versus holistic-inductive designs based on qualitative measurement. The debate and competition between paradigms is best replaced by a new paradigm—a paradigm of choices. The paradigm of choices recognizes that different methods are appropriate for different situations (Patton, 1980). The purpose of this chapter is to describe the qualitative methods option in order to make it more accessible to institutional researchers.

The Nature of Qualitative Data

Qualitative data consist of detailed descriptions of situations, events, people, interactions, and observed behaviors; direct quotations from people about their experiences, attitudes, beliefs, and thoughts; and excerpts or entire passages from documents, correspondence, records, and case histories. The detailed descriptions, direct quotations, and case documentation obtained by qualitative methods are raw data from the empirical world. The data are collected as open-ended narrative. There are no attempts to fit institutional activities or peoples' experiences into predetermined, standardized categories, as the response choices that comprise typical questionnaires or tests do.

Quantitative measurement relies upon instruments that provide a standardized framework in order to limit data collection to certain predetermined response or analysis categories. The experiences of people in institutions and the important variables that describe institutional settings are fit into these standardized categories, to which numerical values are then attached. By contrast, the researcher who uses a qualitative approach seeks to capture what people have to say in their own words. Qualitative data describe the experiences of people in depth. The data are open-ended in order to find out what people's lives, experiences, and interactions mean to them in their own terms and in their natural settings. Qualitative descriptions permit the institutional researcher to record and understand people in their own terms. Qualitative data provide depth and detail. Depth and detail emerge through direct quotation and careful description. The extent of depth and detail will vary, depending upon the nature and purpose of the particular study.

Lofland (1971) has suggested that there are four elements in the collection of qualitative data. First, the qualitative methodologist must get close enough to the people and situation being studied to be able to understand the depth and details of what goes on. Second, the qualitative methodologist must aim at capturing what actually takes place and what people actually say. Third, qualitative data consist of a great deal of pure description of people, activities, and interactions. Fourth, qualitative data consist of direct quotations from people, both what they speak and what they write down. "The commitment to get close, to be factual, descriptive, and quotive, constitutes a significant commitment to represent the participants in their own terms. This does not mean that one becomes an apologist for them but rather that one faithfully depicts what goes on in their lives and what life is like for them, in such a way that one's audience is at least partially able to project themselves into the point of view of the people depicted. They can 'take the role of the other' because the reporter has given them a living sense of day-to-day talk, day-to-day activities, day-to-day concerns and problems. . . . A major methodological consequence of these commitments is that the qualitative study of people in situ is a process of discovery. It is of necessity a process of learning what is happening. Since a major part of what is happening is provided by people in their own terms, one must find out about those terms rather than impose upon them a preconceived or outsider's scheme of what they are about. It is the observer's task to find out what is fundamental or central to the people or world under observation" (Lofland, 1971, p. 4).

Naturalistic Inquiry

Qualitative data emerge from a process of naturalistic inquiry. Qualitative designs are naturalistic in that the researcher does not attempt to manipulate the research setting. The research setting is a naturally occurring event, program, relationship, or interaction that has no predetermined course established by and for the researcher. Rather, the point of using qualitative methods is to understand naturally occurring phenomena in their naturally occurring states.

Willens and Raush (1969, p. 3) define naturalistic inquiry as "the investigation of phenomena within and in relation to their naturally occurring context." In their extensive review of naturalistic inquiry in educational evaluation, Guba and Lincoln (1981) identify two dimensions along which types of scientific inquiry can be described: the extent to which the scientist manipulates some phenomenon in advance in order to study it, and the extent to which constraints are placed on output measures, that is, the extent to which predetermined categories or variables are used to describe the phenomenon under study. They then define "naturalistic inquiry" as a "discovery-oriented" approach that minimizes investigator manipulation of the study setting and places no prior constraints on what the outcomes of the research will be. Naturalistic inquiry is thus contrasted to experimental research, where, ideally, the investigator attempts to control conditions of the study completely by manipulating, changing, or holding constant external influences and where a very limited set of outcome variables is measured.

Wolf and Tymitz (1976–1977, p. 6) describe naturalistic inquiry as an approach aimed at understanding "actualities, social realities, and human perceptions that exist untainted by the obtrusiveness of formal measurement or preconceived questions. It is a process geared to the uncovering of many idiosyncratic but nonetheless important stories told by real people, about real events, in real and natural ways. The more general the provocation, the more these stories will reflect what respondents view as salient issues, meaningful evidence, and appropriate inferences. . . . Naturalistic inquiry attempts to present 'slice-of-life' episodes documented through natural language and representing as closely as possible how people feel, what they know, and what their concerns, beliefs, perceptions, and understandings are."

Under real field conditions, where the researchers wants to know about life and work in institutional settings, naturalistic inquiry replaces the static snapshots of traditional survey research with a dynamic, process orientation. In seeking to understand dynamic processes, the naturalistic inquiry researcher eschews the fixed comparisons of pre-post experimental designs. Instead, the researcher sets out to understand and document the day-to-day reality of the setting or settings under study. The researcher makes no attempt to manipulate, control, or eliminate situational variables or program developments but accepts the complexity of a dynamic institutional reality.

An Inductive Approach

A qualitative research strategy is inductive in that the researcher attempts to make sense of the situation without imposing pre-existing expectations on the research setting. Qualitative designs begin with specific observations and build toward general patterns. Categories or dimensions of analysis emerge from open-ended observations as the researcher comes to understand organizing patterns that exist in the empirical world under study. This contrasts with the hypothetico-deductive approach of experimental designs that require the specification of main variables and the statement of specific research hypotheses before data collection begins. A specification of research hypotheses based on explicit theoretical framework means that general principles provide the framework for understanding specific observations or cases. The researcher must then decide in advance what variables are important and what relationships among those variables can be expected. The strategy in qualitative designs is to allow the important dimensions to emerge from analysis of the cases under study without presupposing in advance what the important dimensions will be. The qualitative methodologist attempts to understand the multiple interrelationships among dimensions that emerge from the data without making prior assumptions about the linear or correlative relationships among narrowly defined, operationalized variables. In short, the inductive approach to institutional research means that an understanding of program activities and outcomes emerges from experience with the setting. Theories about what is happening in a setting are grounded in institutional experience rather than imposed on the setting a priori by hypothetico-deductive constructions.

Institutional research can be inductive in two ways. Within institutions, an inductive approach begins with the individual experiences of participants, without pigeonholing or delimiting what those experiences will be in advance of fieldwork. Between institutions, the inductive approach looks for unique institutional characteristics that make each setting a case unto itself. At either level, generalizations may emerge when case materials are content analyzed, but the initial focus is on full understanding of individual cases, before those unique cases are combined or aggregated. This means that research findings are grounded in specific contexts; the institutional theories that result from the findings will be grounded in real world patterns (Glaser and Strauss, 1967).

A Holistic View of Institutions

The attempt to make sure that institutional analysis is grounded in real world patterns means that qualitative methods require careful specification of the context in which research findings emerge. This contextual sensitivity often involves an effort to develop a holistic view of the institutional setting or settings under analysis. This means that researchers who use qualitative methods strive to understand phenomena and situations as a whole.

The qualitative researcher strives to understand the gestalt, the totality, and the unifying nature of particular settings. The holistic approach assumes that the whole is greater than the sum of its parts; it also assumes that a description and understanding of a program's context is essential for an understanding of the program. Thus, it is insufficient simply to study and measure the parts of a situation by gathering data about isolated variables, scales, or dimensions. In contrast to experimental designs that manipulate and measure the relationships among a few carefully selected and narrowly defined variables, the holistic approach to research design gathers data on any number of aspects of the setting under study in order to assemble a complete picture of the social dynamic of the particular situation or program. This means that, at the time of data collection, each case, event, or setting under study is treated as a unique entity, with its own particular meaning and its own constellation of relationships emerging from and related to the context within which it exists.

Direct Institutional Contact

The methodological mandate to be contextually sensitive, inductive, and naturalistic means that researchers must get close to the phenomenon under study. The institutional researcher who uses qualitative methods attempts to understand the setting under study through direct personal contact and experience with the program. Engaging in holistic-inductive research through naturalistic inquiry represents a comprehensive strategy for describing and understanding institutions that includes specification of the role of the researcher in conduct of the evaluation.

Qualitative research designs require that the researcher get close to the people and situations being studied in order to understand the minutiae of institutional life. The researcher gets close to the institution both through physical proximity for a period of time and through development of closeness in the social sense of intimacy and confidentiality. That many quantitative methodologists fail to ground their findings in qualitative understanding poses what Lofland (1971) calls a major contradiction between their public insistence on the adequacy of statistical portrayals of other humans and their personal, everyday dealings with and judgments about other human beings. "In everyday life, statistical sociologists, like everyone else, assume that they do not know or understand very well people they do not see or associate with very much. They assume that knowing and understanding other people require that one see them reasonably often and in a variety of situations relative to a variety of issues. Moreover, statistical sociologists, like other people, assume that, in order to know or understand others, one is well advised to give some conscious attention to that effort in face-to-face contacts. They assume, too, that the internal world of sociology—or any other social world—is not understandable unless one has been part of it in a face-to-face fashion for quite a period of time. How utterly paradoxical, then, for these same persons to turn around and make, by implication, precisely the opposite claim about people they have never encountered face-to-face—those people appearing as members in their tables and as correlations in their matrices!" (Lofland, 1971, p. 3).

The desire to get close to the situation in order to increase understanding, generate a holistic description of the situation, proceed inductively, and study settings in their naturally occurring complexity "involves the studied commitment to actively enter the worlds of interacting individuals" (Denzin, 1978, pp. 8-9). This makes possible description and understanding of both externally observable behaviors and internal states (world view, opinions, values, attitudes, symbolic constructs). "The inner perspective assumes that understanding can only be achieved by actively participating in the life of the observed and gaining insight by means of introspection" (Bruyn, 1963, p. 226). Actively participating in the life of the observed means, at a minimum, being willing to get close to the sources of data.

The Roots of a Qualitative Research Strategy

This comprehensive strategy of qualitative methods is derived from a variety of philosophical, epistemological, and methodological traditions. Qualitative methods are derived most directly from the ethnographic and field study traditions in anthropology (Pelto and Pelto, 1978), and sociology (Bruyn, 1966). More generally, the holistic-inductive paradigm of naturalistic inquiry is based on perspectives developed in phenomenology (Bussis, Chittenden, and Amarel, 1973; Carini, 1975), symbolic interactionism and naturalistic behaviorism (Denzin, 1978), ethnomethodology (Garfinkel, 1967), and ecological psychology (Barker, 1968). An integrating theme running through these traditions is the fundamental notion or doctrine of *verstehen*. "The basic dispute clustering around the notion of *verstehen* has typically sounded something like the following: The advocate of some version of the *verstehen* doctrine will claim that human beings can be understood in a manner that other objects of study cannot. Men have purposes and emotions, they make plans, construct cultures, and hold certain values, and their behavior is influenced by such values, plans, and purposes. In short, a human being lives in a world which has 'meaning' to him, and, because his behavior has meaning, human actions are intelligible in ways that the behavior of nonhuman objects is not. The opponents of this view. . . will maintain that human behavior is to be explained in the same manner as is the behavior of other objects of nature. There are laws governing human behavior. An action is explained when it can be subsumed under some such law, and, of course, such laws are confirmed by empirical evidence" (Strike, 1972, p. 28).

The *verstehen* approach assumes that the social sciences need methods different from those used in agricultural experimentation and natural science, because human beings are different from plants and nuclear particles. The *verstehen* tradition stresses understanding that focuses on the meaning of human behavior, the context of social interaction, an empathetic understanding based on subjective experience, and the connections between subjective states and behavior. The *verstehen* tradition places emphasis on the human capacity to know and understand others through sympathetic introspection and reflection on detailed description and observation.

Bogdan and Taylor (1975) contrast the *verstehen* tradition rooted in phenomenology to logical positivism, the dominant social science perspective in the twentieth century: "Two major theoretical perspectives have dominated the social science scene. One, *positivism,* traces its origins to the great social theorists of the nineteenth and early twentieth centuries and especially to August Comte and Emile Durkheim. The positivist seeks the *facts* or *causes* of social phenomena with little regard for the subjective states of individuals. Durkheim advises the social scientist to consider 'social facts,' or social phenomena, as 'things' that exercise an external and coercive force on human behavior. The second theoretical perspective, which, following the lead of Irwin Deutscher, we will describe as *phenomenological,* stems most prominently from Max Weber. The phenomenologist is concerned with *understanding* human behavior from the actor's own frame of reference. . . . The phenomenologist examines how the world is experienced. For him or her, the important reality is what people imagine it to be. *Since the positivists and the phenomenologists approach different problems and seek different answers, their research will typically demand different methodologies"* (Bogdan and Taylor, 1975, p. 2; italics in the original).

The phenomenological tradition in qualitative methods proposes an active, involved role for the institutional researcher. "Hence, insight may be regarded as the core of social knowledge. It is arrived at by being on the inside of the phenomena to be observed. . . . It is participation in an activity that generates interest, purpose, point of view, value, meaning, and intelligibility, as well as bias" (Wirth, 1949, p. xxii).

This is a quite different scientific process from that envisioned by the classical, experimental approach to science. "This in no way suggests that the researcher lacks the ability to be scientific while collecting the data. On the contrary, it merely specifies that it is crucial for validity—and, consequently, for reliability—to try to picture the empirical social world as it actually exists to those under investigation rather than as the researcher imagines it to be" (Filstead, 1970, p. 4).

The importance of such field techniques as participant observation, in-depth interviewing, detailed description, and qualitative field notes derives from these philosophical and epistemological assumptions.

Practical Qualitative Approaches

Holistic-inductive research through naturalistic inquiry is a strategic ideal. In conceptualization, a pure qualitative methods strategy emphasizes a holistic approach, where the researcher neither manipulates the setting under study nor predetermines what variables or categories are worth measuring. In practice, however, it is important to recognize that holistic-inductive analysis and naturalistic inquiry are always a matter of degree. In making this point, Guba (1978) has depicted the practice of naturalistic inquiry as a wave on which the investigator moves from varying degrees of a "discovery mode" to varying emphasis on a "verification mode." As the research begins, the investigator is open to whatever emerges from the data—a discovery or inductive approach. Then, as the inquiry reveals patterns and major dimensions of interest, the investigator begins to focus on verifying and elucidating what appears to be emerging—a deductive approach to data collection and analysis.

In the same vein, the attempt to understand an institution as a whole in a context does not mean that the investigator never becomes involved in component analysis and never looks at particular variables, dimensions, and parts of a program as separate entities. Rather, it means that the qualitative methodologist consciously works back and forth between parts and wholes, separate variables, and complex, interwoven constellations of variables in a sorting-out, putting-together process. Guided by a strategy that mandates striving to present a contextually sensitive picture of the institution, the qualitative researcher recognizes that certain periods during data collection and analysis can focus on component, variable, and less-than-the-whole kinds of analysis.

The practice and practicalities of field work also mean that the strategic mandate to get close to the institution or setting under study is not absolute and fixed. Closeness to and involvement with the program under study are most usefully viewed as variable dimensions. The personal styles and capabilities of researchers permit and necessitate variance along these dimensions. Variations in type of studies and research purposes affect the extent to which the researcher can or ought to get close to institutional members. Moreover, closeness is likely to vary over the course of the study. At times, the researcher can become totally immersed in the institutional experience. These periods of immersion can be followed by times of withdrawal and distance (for personal as well as for methodological reasons), which are followed by new experiences of immersion in and intimacy with the setting.

Qualitative methods can be used both to discover what is happening and to verify what has been discovered. What is discovered must be verified by going back to the empirical world under study and examining the extent to which the emergent analysis fits the phenomenon and works to explain what has been observed. Glaser and Strauss (1967, p. 3) describe what it means for results to fit and work. "By *fit* we mean that the categories must be readily (not forcibly) applicable to and indicated by the data under study; by *work* we mean that they must be meaningfully relevant to and be able to explain the behavior under study." Discovery and verification mean moving back and forth between induction and deduction, between experience and reflection on experience, and between greater and lesser degrees of naturalistic inquiry.

The practical tactics of qualitative methods do not undermine the strategic ideals of qualitative research. Those strategic ideals provide the basic framework out of which practical tactics are developed and in which actual field procedures are grounded. Holistic-inductive analysis based on naturalistic inquiry constitutes the strategy of qualitative methods that provide a framework for and guidance in making practical, tactical decisions about any particular study.

References

Barker, R. G. *Ecological Psychology.* Stanford, Calif.: Stanford University Press, 1968.

Bogdan, R., and Taylor, S. J. *Introduction to Qualitative Methods.* New York: Wiley, 1975.

Bruyn, S. "The Methodology of Participant Observation." *Human Organization,* 1963, *21,* 224–235.

Bruyn, S. *The Human Perspective in Sociology: The Methodology of Participant Observation.* Englewood Cliffs, N.J.: Prentice-Hall, 1966.

Bussis, A., Chittenden, E. A., and Amarel, M. "Methodology in Educational Evaluation and Research." Unpublished mimeograph, Educational Testing Service.

Carini, P. F. *Observation and Description: An Alternative Methodology for the Investigation of Human Phenomena.* North Dakota Study Group on Evaluation Monograph Series. Grand Forks: University of North Dakota, 1975.

Denzin, N. K. "The Logic of Naturalistic Inquiry." N. K. Denzin (Ed.), *Sociological Methods: A Sourcebook.* New York: McGraw-Hill, 1978.

Denzin, N. K. *The Research Act.* New York: McGraw-Hill, 1978.

Filstead, W. J. (Ed.). *Qualitative Methodology.* Chicago: Markham, 1970.

Garfinkel, H. *Studies in Ethnomethodology.* Englewood Cliffs, N.J.: Prentice-Hall, 1967.

Glaser, B. G., and Strauss, A. L. *Discovery of Grounded Strategies for Qualitative Research.* Chicago: Aldine, 1967.

Guba, E. G. *Toward a Methodology of Naturalistic Inquiry in Educational Evaluation.* CSE Monograph Series in Evaluation, No. 8. Los Angeles: Center for the Study of Evaluation, University of California at Los Angeles, 1978.

Guba, E. G., and Lincoln, Y. *Effective Evaluation: Improving the Usefulness of Evaluation Results Through Responsive and Naturalistic Approaches.* San Francisco: Jossey-Bass, 1981.

Kuhn, T. *The Structure of Scientific Revolutions.* Chicago: University of Chicago Press, 1970.

Lofland, J. *Analyzing Social Settings.* Belmont, Calif.: Wadsworth, 1971.

Patton, M. Q. *Utilization-Focused Evaluation.* Beverly Hills, Calif.: Sage, 1978.

Patton, M. Q. *Qualitative Evaluation Methods.* Beverly Hills, Calif.: Sage, 1980.

Patton, M. Q. *Creative Evaluation.* Beverly Hills, Calif.: Sage, 1981.

Pelto, P. J., and Pelto, G. H. *Anthropological Research: The Structure of Inquiry.* Cambridge: Cambridge University Press, 1978.

Strike, K. "Explaining and Understanding: The Impact of Science On Our Concept of Man." In L. G. Thomas (Ed.), *Philosophical Redirection of Educational Research: The 71st Yearbook of the National Society for the Study of Education.* Chicago: University of Chicago Press, 1972.

Willens, E. P., and Raush, H. L. *Naturalistic Viewpoints in Psychological Research.* New York: Holt, Rinehart and Winston, 1969.

Wolf, R. L., and Tymitz, B. "Ethnography and Reading: Matching Inquiry Mode to Process." *Reading Research Quarterly,* 1976–1977, *12,* 5–11.

Wirth, L. "Preface." In K. Mannheim, *Ideology and Utopia.* New York: Harcourt Brace Jovanovich, 1949.

Michael Quinn Patton is director of the Minnesota Center for Social Research and an adjunct professor in the Hubert H. Humphrey Institute of Public Affairs, University of Minnesota, where he was named outstanding teacher of the year in 1976. This chapter was written while Dr. Patton served as team leader for an evaluation and planning project at the University of the West Indies, Trinidad, involving agricultural development in nine Caribbean countries.

*In the social sciences, thin descriptions abound
and find their expression in correlation
coefficients, path diagrams, F-ratios, dummy
variables, structural equations, tests of
significance, and social indicators.*

Contributions of Anthropology and Sociology to Qualitative Research Methods

Norman K. Denzin

Qualitative research methods, as employed by interpretive anthropologists and sociologists (Becker, 1970; Bluebond-Langner, 1978; Blumer, 1969; Geertz, 1973; Glaser and Strauss, 1967; Manners and Kaplan, 1968; Wax, 1971), call for the close-up inspection of ongoing human group life. These methods demand a commitment to enter actively the worlds of those studied so as to render those worlds understandable within an interpretive framework that is grounded in the behaviors, interactions, languages, meanings, symbolic forms, and emotions of those studied. Within an institutional or organizational context (Denzin, 1979), these methods are fitted to the social worlds and spheres of interaction that constitute the everyday life of the organization or institution under study.

Portions of this discussion have been worked out in conversations with Richard Herbert Howe.

E. Kuhns, S. V. Martorana (Eds.). *New Directions for Institutional Research: Qualitative Methods for Institutional Research*, no. 34. San Francisco: Jossey-Bass, March 1982.

Rich, thickly textured ethnographic descriptions of the subject's life world within group and institutional arenas provide a point of departure for the qualitative researcher. (On thick description, see Coles, 1977; Geertz, 1973; and Ryle, 1968; see Braudel, 1975, for the classic demonstration of this methodological strategy.)

In this chapter, the forms of qualitative research currently employed in anthropology and sociology will be briefly reviewed. Particular emphasis will be placed on the research strategies of participant observation, life history and case study construction, open-ended interviewing, and collection of behavior specimens. While the basic assumptions of these methods will be discussed and their relevance for institutional and organizational studies will be addressed, my primary concern rests with the development of what can be termed *interpretive evaluation,* which is to be distinguished from evaluation research. The focus on evaluation is justified on two grounds. First, the implications of qualitative research methods for evaluation studies is just beginning to be developed in the literature (Patton, 1980). Secondly, the application of these methods in institutional settings is as yet not well understood (Denzin, 1979; Patton, 1980).

Qualitative Research Strategies

Participant observation represents a synthesis of the major forms of qualitative research strategies. It can be defined as a field strategy that simultaneously combines open-ended interviewing, document analysis, and life history construction with participation and observation in the worlds studied. As a strategy, this method throws the researcher directly into the life world under investigation, and it requires the careful recording through field notes of the problematic and routine features of that world. Recurring structural, interactional, and meaning patterns are sought. Sometimes, as in Cavan's (1974) study of a "hippie" community in Northern California, this method includes the gathering of materials on kinship, economic, political, religious, linguistic, and artistic structures. In Howe's (1979) study of the early office proletariat, research involved the historical and phenomenological reconstruction of the flow of an order-processing system through a division of labor within the Sears mail-order house in Chicago around 1910. In these cases, the analyst attempts to discover and give meaning to the embodied, embedded, and situated practices that participants in the world find themselves caught up in and committed to. The meaning that is given to the practices, consistent with Weber's (1977) directives, must flow from the life world of the participants and not be attached a priori by the interpreter.

In some cases, the participant observer is a known observer. In others, the observer attempts to enter the world as a participant without disclosing observational intentions (Gold, 1958). In all cases, the researcher attempts to share in the subject's world, to directly participate in the rounds of activities that make up that world, and to see the world as the subject sees it. The participant observer's goals revolve around the attempt to render that world meaningful from the perspective of those studied.

Life history research presents the experiences and meanings held by a single individual, a group, or an organization. Life history materials include records or documents that shed light on the subjective behaviors and interpretations of individuals or groups (Denzin, 1978). Some life histories attempt to cover the entire sweep of an individual's, institution's, or a group's life course. Others are topical in nature, pertaining only to a specific range of perhaps predefined experiences, such as a juvenile delinquent's moral career through the social welfare and correctional establishments. Life histories endeavor to weave individual history into social history, thereby linking private problems with their public institutional representations (Mills, 1958). The goal of life history research is to record in an unfolding fashion the experiences of a person or group over a period of time, so as to render those experiences subjectively understandable. The real, actual, or objective meanings of those experiences as seen from another perspective are not of central concern to the life history investigator.

Open-ended interviewing requires working from a general list of information that the researcher wants or from a set of questions for which the researcher wishes answers. These questions are put to those studied in the manner of a focused interview (Merton and Kendall, 1946). The phrasing of the questions and the order in which they are asked are altered to fit each individual. Open-ended interviewing assumes that meanings, understandings, and interpretations cannot be standardized; they cannot be obtained with a formal, fixed-choice questionnaire. Open-ended interviewing assumes a skilled asker of questions, and it presumes skill in listening. The strategy fits naturally with participant observation and life history analysis, and in practice it cannot be separated from these two methods.

Behavior specimens are slices of ongoing interaction taken from natural, recurring social situations. Specimens can be drawn from arenas as diverse as lunchtime in a day care center and the firing of an employee in a corporation. In presenting a behavior specimen, the researcher should give each interactant a short biography relevant to the situation at hand. The situation of interaction should be detailed, as should the objects acted on. The relationships that obtain between the interactants should be indicated. Most importantly, the actual sequence of conversation and interaction should be recorded and presented (Denzin, 1978).

Behavior specimens are much like the field notes of an ethnographer. If carefully prepared, they ensure that the researcher leaves the field situation with a full account of the interactions that have taken place. The specimen gives a fine-grained record of social interaction in natural social situations.

Participant observation, life history research, open-ended interviewing, and collection of behavior specimens represent the fundamental tools of the qualitative researcher. Analytically, they are inseparable. They should be regarded as interrelated strategies which move the researcher directly into the worlds of those studied.

Evaluational Criteria

Elsewhere (Denzin, 1978), I have reviewed the matters of reliability, external and internal validity, sampling representativeness, generalizability, causal adequacy, and causal analysis and suggested strategies for confronting these traditional quantitative questions. In this chapter, I will address the questions of authenticity, thick description, and verisimilitude. Traditional positivistic, quantitative criteria of evaluation are not relevant when the investigator is committed to the qualitative study of everyday life.

Authenticity raises the criterion of lived relevance. Are the researcher's observations and records grounded in the natural, everyday language, behaviors, meanings, and interactions of those studied? If they are authentically real, the world of the subject speaks through the researcher's document (Merleau-Ponty, 1973). An authentic document discloses the hiddenness of the world and reveals its underlying problematics and the structures that are taken for granted (Heidegger, 1962).

An authentic document rests on thick description. Thick description can be defined, in part, by its contrast with thin description. Ryle (1968) provides an example of thin description: "You hear someone come out with 'Today is the third of February.' What is he doing? Obviously, the thinnest possible description of what he is doing would fit a gramophone equally well, that he was launching this sequence of syllables into the air" (Ryle, 1968, pp. 8–9). A thick description goes beyond fact to detail, context, emotion, and webs of relationship. In a thick description, the voices, feelings, and meanings of persons are heard. In the social sciences, thin descriptions abound and find their expression in correlation coefficients, path diagrams, F-ratios, dummy variables, structural equations, tests of significance, and social indicators. Thick descriptions are exceedingly rare, yet they are the stuff of interpretation and qualitative evaluation in the social sciences.

Verisimilitude derives from authentic, thick descriptions. It is achieved when the author of a document brings the life world alive in the mind of the reader. The intent of verisimilitude is to convey that the experiences recorded and experienced by the observer would have been sensed by the reader, had he been present during the actual moments of interaction that are reflected in the document.

Interpretive Evaluation Versus Evaluation Research

In its various conceptualizations, evaluation research rests on the assumption that treatment programs, experimentally and quasi-experimentally defined, have effects on real world affairs that can objectively be determined through the quantitative manipulation of data drawn from the world under study. By objectifying the observational process, this model divorces the researcher from the world under investigation. The model presumes that intervention programs are static and reflect a strict cause and effect paradigm. It is assumed that the causal effects of the program can be identified beforehand by the investigator. The worlds, meanings, and interpretations of the subject are not given primary attention in the traditional evaluation research design. The evaluations that occur within such designs are not clearly aimed at determining how the programs enter into, create, destroy, alter, shape, or modify the life worlds of the persons whom they are intended to benefit.

Interpretive evaluation research assumes that the interpretations and evaluations given to programs in the real world are ongoing, subject to continual interpretation, evaluation, and negotiation. Effects, evaluations, and interpretations are not one-time occurrences, nor can their effects be captured through follow-up studies that presume to objectify the realities under examination through retesting. Interpretive evaluation assumes that the "fore-understandings" that investigators have of the worlds that they examine must slowly be lifted and fitted into the interpretive process. That is, "inquiry itself is the behavior of a questioner" (Heidegger, 1962, p. 24). The basic concepts that the investigator brings to an investigation must be seen as part of the research, and they "determine the way in which we get an understanding beforehand of the area of the subject-matter . . . . all positive investigation is guided by this understanding" (Heidegger, 1962, p. 30). Every inquiry is guided beforehand by what is sought (Heidegger, 1962, p. 24). Accordingly, the interpretive scheme that an analyst brings to an evaluation project is part of the evaluation. A hermeneutic circle of interpretation underlies the evaluation process. Heidegger states: "This circle of understanding is not an orbit in which any random kind of knowledge may move; it is the expression of the existential forestructure of Dasein itself. It is not to be reduced to the level of a vicious circle or even of a circle which is merely tolerated. . . . What is decisive is not to get out of the circle but to come into it the right way" (Heidegger, 1962, p. 195). Quantitative evaluation research has historically attempted to break out of the circle of interpretation so as to produce objective evaluations of occurrences in the real world. Such evaluations have foundered because those who made them have not known how (or perhaps not been willing) to enter into the circle of understanding that stands at the heart of interpretive, qualitative evaluation research.

Interpretive evaluation enters this circle by placing the investigator squarely in the center of the research process. The methods of participant observation outlined earlier are basic to all interpretation (Stone, 1981). The world of interpretation does not reveal itself as causes and effects. Rather, it becomes apparent and visible through the voices and interactions of everyday individuals. Interpretive evaluation seeks not to evaluate so much as to reveal and disclose, to reveal the world as felt, lived, and experienced by those studied. It speaks through the languages and conceptual categories of ordinary people. It studies the world in terms of the embodied, embedded, situated practices of these people and attempts to uncover the structures and meanings that lie behind these practices.

The everyday scientific notions of objectivity and subjectivity are set aside in interpretive studies. The fallacy of objectivism that underlies most quantitative research fosters the illusion that the researcher can somehow stand apart from the worlds under study. Subject and object dissolve within the circle of understanding as the investigator attempts to disclose and uncover the interactional experiences of those studied. In so doing, the observer, as a participant in interpretation, becomes a part of the world that is interpreted.

The aims of interpretive evaluation are neither generalizing nor nomothetic. They are, rather, descriptive and particularizing, aimed at revealing life experiences in concrete social situations where interpretation, understanding, and evaluation are ordinary, everyday activities. In short, this method seeks to return interpretation and evaluation to their natural home, the everyday life world. The interpretive schemes of everyday people are sought in these investigations, and the interpretive theories of the social scientists are set aside once the investigation begins.

Power, History, Emotion, and Knowledge

Qualitative, interpretive evaluation research is guided by one question: How is the life world shaped, controlled, and constrained by applied programs and by the decisions of persons in decision-making positions? The analysis of power, history, emotion, meaning, and force is central in answering this question.

History enters qualitative interpretation simply because the events and processes that research interprets unfold over time, assuming, as Braudel (1975) argues, the essential features of both short-term and long-term events. In the short term, persons attempt to make their own history, in the face of the histories that are pressed onto them by those in decision making positions. In the long run, history takes and moves its own course, and the interpretations of people simply become part of the historical picture. A time span that sweeps one or two hundred years engulfs the tiny interpretive strands that persons collectively and individually have constructed. Smaller time periods—one year, five years, a decade, perhaps—stand out with their dominant interpretive paradigms.

All evaluation research must be adjusted to an interpretive structure that renders time meaningful to the people and events studied. Too often, the artificial constraints of research design ignore the temporal parameters of the phenomenon being interpreted and evaluated. As a consequence, the evaluation product seems trivial.

Power permeates every structure of a society. Power is embedded in the microrelations that make up everyday life (Foucault, 1980). It is present in the situated practices and the artful productions of everyday routines. Neither an object nor a force to be applied, power is in the person and is part of these situated practices that the person lays claim to and calls *mine.* Whether the doings are tool-using, knowledge-making, or product-using, the situated practices of everyday life involve persons acting "as if" they were controlling their own activities and affairs. How persons construct and act on such constructions involves a central focus of interpretive inquiry.

Close inspection reveals that persons invest their everyday worlds with mood, feeling, and emotion. In this invested feeling, they display those "as if" actions that place them in control of their own and others' destinies. The anatomy of power and feeling in society (both at hand and at large) deprives quantitative evaluation research of detached, objective knowledge of the life world. For, as Foucault argues, "Knowledge derives not from some subject of knowledge but from the power relations that invest it. . . . Knowledge cannot be neutral, pure. All knowledge is political . . . because knowledge has its conditions of possibility in power relations. No science can create its own conditions of possibility. . . . Political anatomy deprives science of its own foundations" (Sheridan, 1980, p. 220).

Under the positivist paradigm, quantitative, applied, and evaluative knowledge is assumed to be objectively valid. Under the interpretive qualitative paradigm, knowledge can be assumed neither to be objective nor to be valid in any objective sense. Rather, knowledge reflects interpretive structures and the power relations that permeate a society. As a consequence, the interpretive and qualitative methods of anthropology and sociology reveal not objective reality but the interpreted worlds of interacting individuals. These worlds, it must be concluded, are the only worlds an interpretive discipline can assume.

Conclusion

Detached evaluations have been situated in this discussion. They represent the embodied and embedded practices of a group of scientific practitioners. The work of this group reflects power relations in society at large. The knowledge that is produced by these practices is not objective, nor is it necessarily valid or pragmatically useful. If one's goal is the understanding and interpretation of the world as it is lived, experienced, and practiced, then the methodological strategies discussed in this chapter seem warranted.

References

Becker, H. S. *Sociological Work*. Chicago: Aldine, 1970.

Bluebond-Langner, M. *The Private Worlds of Dying Children*. Princeton, N.J.: Princeton University Press, 1978.

Blumer, H. *Symbolic Interactionism*. Englewood Cliffs, N.J.: Prentice-Hall, 1969.

Braudel, F. *The Mediterranean and the Mediterranean World in the Age of Philip II*. New York: Harper, 1975.

Cavan, S. "Seeing Social Structure in a Rural Setting." *Urban Life and Culture*, 1974, *3*, 329–346.

Coles, R. *Privileged Ones: The Well-Off and the Rich in America*. Boston: Little, Brown, 1977.

Denzin, N. K. *The Research Act*. (2nd ed.) New York: McGraw-Hill, 1978.

Denzin, N. K. "The Interactionist Study of Social Organization: A Note on Method." *Symbolic Interaction*, 1979, 2, 59–72.

Foucault, M. *Power/Knowledge: Selected Interviews and Other Writings, 1972–1977*. New York: Pantheon Books, 1980.

Geertz, C. *The Interpretation of Culture*. New York: Basic Books, 1973.

Glaser, B., and Strauss, A. *The Discovery of Grounded Theory*. Chicago: Aldine, 1967.

Gold, R. "Roles in Sociological Field Observations." *Social Forces*, 1958, *36*, 217–223.

Heidegger, M. *Being and Time*. New York: Harper, 1962.

Howe, R. H. "Early Office Proletariat? A Reconstruction of Sear's Order Processing 1910." In N. K. Denzin (Ed.), *Studies in Symbolic Interaction: A Research Annual*, vol. 5. Greenwich, Conn.: JAI Press, forthcoming.

Manners, R. O., and Kaplan, D. (Eds.). *Theory in Anthropology: A Sourcebook*. Chicago: Aldine, 1968.

Merleau-Ponty, M. "The Prose of the World." Evanston, Ill.: Northwestern University Press, 1973.

Merton, R. K., and Kendall, P. "The Focused Interview." *American Journal of Sociology*, 1946, *51*, 541–557.

Mills, C. W. *The Sociological Imagination*. New York: Oxford University Press, 1958.

Patton, M. Q. *Qualitative Evaluation Methods*. Beverly Hills, Calif.: Sage, 1980.

Ryle, G. *The Thinking of Thoughts*. Saskatoon: University of Saskatchewan University Lectures, No. 18, 1968.

Sheridan, A. *Michel Foucault: The Will to Truth*. New York: Tavistock, 1980.

Stone, B. L. "Towards a Hermeneutic of Meaningful Social Action," Unpublished doctoral dissertation, Department of Sociology, University of Illinois, Urbana, 1981.

Wax, R. *Doing Fieldwork*. Chicago: University of Chicago Press, 1971.

Weber, M. *Critique of Stammler*. (E. Oakes, Trans.) New York: Free Press, 1977.

Norman K. Denzin is a professor of sociology at
the University of Illinois, Urbana. He is the author
of Childhood Socialization *(Jossey-Bass, 1977),*
The Research Act, *2nd ed. (McGraw-Hill, 1978), and*
a forthcoming monograph on interpretation in
the social sciences.

Mathematicians are finding a new vocabulary useful in bridging the gap between institutional data, which are difficult to measure, and social interactions, which are difficult to compute.

Contributions of Mathematics to Qualitative Research Methods

F. Craig Johnson
R. C. Lacher

Three people from the same university meet in a bar after work, and, as their shoptalk mellows, they begin to share their opinions of each other. The analyst from the institutional research office says to the president's assistant, "The information you give to the president to help him make his decisions has to be irrational and unscientific, because your measurements are based upon such vague indices." To which the president's assistant replies, "Your analysis is of little help to us, because your measurements are so restrictive that they describe only a tiny part of the problem." At this point, a mathematics professor intervenes to say, "Your models are diffeomorphic and therefore share the same diffeomorphism invariants or qualitative properties." After a thoughtful pause, the talk shifts to football, since no one seems to have any idea what the others are talking about.

In this chapter, these three points of view will be explored, and the suggestion will be made that a qualitative language needs

E. Kuhns, S. V. Martorana (Eds.). *New Directions for Institutional Research: Qualitative Methods for Institutional Research*, no. 34. San Francisco: Jossey-Bass, March 1982.

to be learned in order to improve communication. This language has a new vocabulary and a grammar. Once this language is learned, we will make an application to institutional research, showing how problems that so far have been insoluble can be clarified by reducing the arbitrariness of description.

Definitions

These are some terms of the new vocabulary: *qualitative, dynamical systems, local maxima* and *minima, delay rule, Maxwell's rule, voting rule, steepest ascent, bifurcation, hysteresis, saddle point, cusp catastrophe,* and *vector field.* Some terms used to describe the grammar rules, like *parameterized* and *coordinatized,* may seem strange to the nonmathematician, but we have elected to use them rather than the four- or five-word paraphrase. The grammar rules are the postulates, assumptions, and hypotheses that form the qualitative model. We must remember that the models are related to reality only to the extent that the assumptions and hypotheses are related to reality. With this warning in mind, the dynamical systems model can be a useful tool for thinking about problems in a qualitative way.

Qualitative. Let x, x' be two one-dimensional scales describing the same data. If the change of scale from x to x' and the change from x' back to x is smooth and order-preserving, that is $\frac{dx'}{dx} > 0$ for all x, then the scales x and x' are said to be *qualitatively related.* Any statement based upon the particular scale x is called *qualitatively* invariant if the same statement can be made about every scale x' qualitatively related to x. Qualitatively invariant conclusions are called *qualitative conclusions* (Zeeman, 1977).

Dynamical Systems. A dynamic system consists of a number of states, $x = (x^{(1)}, \ldots, x^{(n)})$ and rules governing changes of state. The rules may be thought of as differential equations in the form

$$\frac{dx}{dt}(i) = f_j(x^{(1)}, \ldots, x^{(n)})$$

where f_j ($j = , \ldots, n$) are smooth functions of n variables, and t represents time. In contrast to a system of differential equations, the rules for a dynamical system can be taken to specify speed for each point x in the phase space, with these specifications being smooth functions of x. A parameterized dynamical system is really an entire collection of dynamical systems parameterized by one or more real parameters $c^{(1)}, \ldots, c^{(n)}$, which are often referred to as *external* or *control* parameters. Many of the dynamically less-complicated concepts of this theory can be illustrated by a model of decision making for a college or a university (Zeeman, 1977).

Qualitative Model

It is difficult for the authors to imagine a deterministic system in any setting—physical, biological, or social—that is not accurately modeled by some parameterized dynamical discrete-time system. Therefore, unless dynamical systems phenomena are ruled out on scientific grounds, they must be considered at least potentially useful in understanding real data in higher education (Zeeman, 1977). The following model is presented in a form directed not toward mathematical elegance but toward intuitive understanding.

In a decision-making model, there is explicit description of probability of the opinion x, the potential function $P_{a,b,}(x)$, splitting factors, and other things that can be collected by a suitably designed questionnaire. What is implicit in the model is the underlying dynamic representing the influence of communication on people as they make up their minds. Consider a college or university with an administration that both wants to please its students, faculty, and alumni and is afraid of change. Specifically, assume that there is an entire range of options for an admissions policy, parameterized by one or more numerical coordinates x, and that the administration has opinion-gathering techniques that accurately discover the distribution of opinion relative to these options. Assume, further, that postulates 1–3 hold.

Postulate 1: Admissions standards will be set at a local maximum of the opinion distribution.

For example, if the distribution looks like

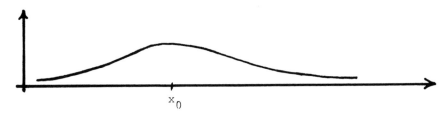

x_0

with a (local) maximum occurring at $x = x_0$ and no other local maxima, then policy will be set at x_0. If the distribution looks like

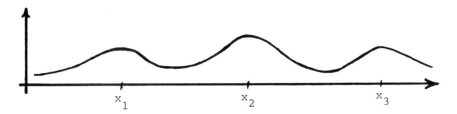

then policy will be at either x_1, x_2, or x_3. Local maxima of the distribution can be referred to as *opinion bases* or simply as bases. Postulate 1 is a consequence of the administration's desire to please its students, faculty, and alumni.

Postulate 2: Once set, the admissions policy will remain at an opinion base (local maximum) as long as that base exists.

Thus, if policy is set at x_1, based on yesterday's distribution

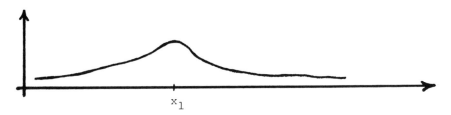

but today's distribution looks like

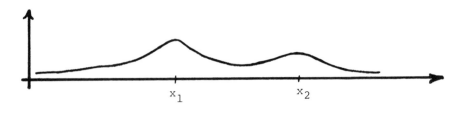

policy will remain at x_1. Even if the distributions change over time to something like

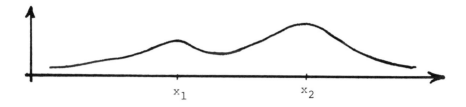

policy will remain at x_1.

Postulate 2 is called the *delay rule*. Two other possibilities in this setting are *Maxwell's rule,* which states that policy changes whenever necessary in order to be where support peaks the highest, and the *voting rule,* which places policy at the peak with greatest area. We chose the delay rule for two reasons: It embodies the concept of fear of change (administrative inertia), and it is a mathematical property of all gradient dynamical systems.

Postulate 3: If the admissions policy is set at an opinion base (local maximum) that disappears, policy will be changed to a new base. Whenever possible, this new base is selected by *steepest ascent* of the opinion distribution.

Locating the steepest ascent of the opinion distribution $P(x)$ means following the trajectories of the differential equation $\frac{dx}{dt} = \nabla P(x)$, where $\nabla P(x)$ is the gradient vector of P at x. Some examples help to clarify postulate 3.

Example 1: Suppose opinion changes over time as follows:

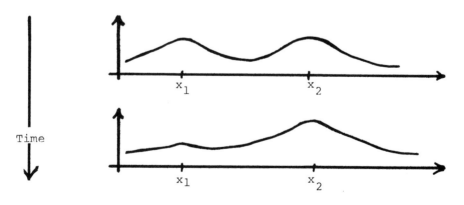

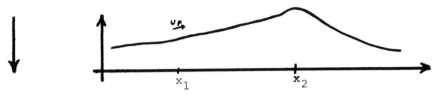

If policy is set at x_1, then the base for the current admissions policy shrinks and finally disappears. At the time of disappearance, the new admissions policy is reset at x_2, since going "up" the distribution from x_1 (at the time x_1 ceases to locate a local maximum) forces motion toward the local maximum x_2.

Example 2: Stationary bifurcation

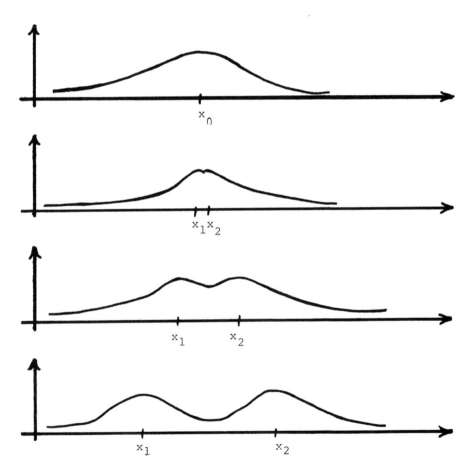

As one maximum divides into two, policy makers must choose to follow one. Which one is not covered by the postulates.

Example 3: Hysteresis loop

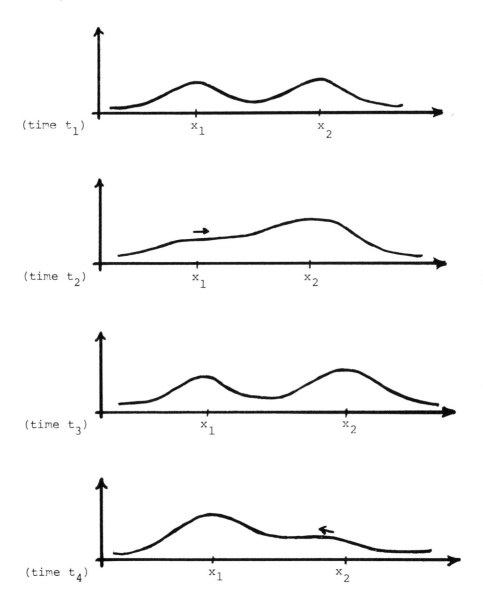

(time t_1) x_1 x_2

(time t_2) x_1 x_2

(time t_3) x_1 x_2

(time t_4) x_1 x_2

Note: At time t_5, the distribution has returned to a configuration like time t_1.

With an admissions policy set at x_1, loss of opinion base at x_1 forces a shift of policy to x_2. Then a base reappears at x_1 while the base at x_2 disappears, forcing a shift back to x_1.

34

Example 4: Saddle point. When the range of options is parameterized by two independent coordinates $x = (x^{(1)}, x^{(2)})$, the distribution of opinion looks like a landscape, with peaks, pits, and passes. The peaks are the local maxima, so policy must be set at a peak. A saddle point dilemma can occur when loss of support base for the current admissions policy (that is, disappearance of the peak at which policy is set) forces the administration to seek another policy by steepest ascent of the landscape. If the path of steepest ascent leads directly to a pass, a saddle point dilemma presents itself to the administration: It is not a peak, but it has no criteria with which to choose one of the peaks adjacent to the pass. See Figure 1.

Figure 1. Saddlepoint

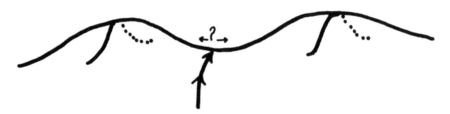

Example 5: Cusp catastrophe. More than one parameter maybe involved in the evolving opinion distribution. When there is only one such parameter, it is convenient to think of this parameter as time, as we have done in examples 1–4. Note, however, that a more fundamental parameter is implied in example 3, since the distribution returns to its t_1 state at time t_4, even though time itself is irreversible. In the case of two parameters affecting the opinion distribution, we will not think of either as time per se, although both parameters can be functions of time. Examples of such parameters include age or wealth of the population, perceived threat, and perceived prospects for gain.

In the case where two independent parameters determine the opinion distribution, it may be that one of these parameters induces bifurcation behavior, as in example 2, and the other induces hysteresis loop behavior, as in example 3. The behavior of our model under both parameters simultaneously is often described as a cusp catastrophe.

Figure 2. Cust Catastrophe

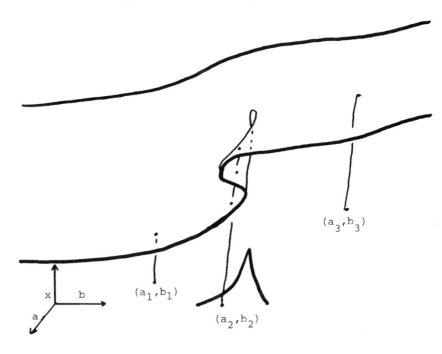

(a_3, b_3)

x   b

a

(a_1, b_1)

(a_2, b_2)

The word *cusp* arises from the graph consisting of all maxima and minima of the distribution plotted over a plane coordinatized by the two parameters in question. That is, given a value for
each of the two parameters (*a* and *b*, say), there is at least one
maximum of the distribution, and this maximum, along with all
the other maxima and minima of this particular distribution, is
plotted over the point (*a*, *b*). The resulting graph appears as a surface in space parameterized by *a*, *b*, *x*. A canonical representation is
depicted in Figure 2.

Consider the points (a_1, b_1) and (a_2, b_2) in the ab-plane of
Figure 2. There is only one point of the surface over (a_1, b_1), indicating that there is only one maximum, and no minimum, of the
distribution when $a = a_1$, $b = b_1$. There are three points of the surface over (a_2, b_2), indicating two maxima separated by a minimum
in the distribution when $a = a_2$, $b = b_2$. The region in the ab-plane
over which the surface is multiple valued [as over (a_2, b_2)] we will
call the *cusp region*. Bifurcation occurs, just as in example 2, when
the parameters (*a*, *b*) follow a path into the cusp region through
the cusp point. A hysteresis loop occurs, just as in example 3, when

the parameters (a, b) follow a path leading from one side of the cusp region into the cusp region, out the other side, and back again.

The Model as Dynamical System. The precise meaning of steepest ascent was given in terms of the parameterized dynamical system

$$\frac{dx}{dt} = \nabla P(x) \qquad (*)$$

where P is the parameterized distribution of opinion, and x represents a possible multidimensional option of policy. In essence, the gradient of P is a *vector field* on P that points in the steepest ascent direction. The three postulates can be restated in terms of this system.

Postulate 1: Admissions policy will be set at a stable equilibrium of (*).

Postulate 2: Admissions policy will tend to remain in a stable equilibrium as long as that equilibrium remains stable.

Postulate 3: When forced to change, admissions policy will follow trajectories of (*), so far as possible, toward a new stable equilibrium.

Intelligence. This model presents a simplified picture of some of the problems that algorithmic administration of colleges and universities can encounter. Of course, most colleges and universities require intelligence on the part of their leadership. Even in this simplified model, such intelligence must be invoked at points of bifurcation, or saddle points, in order to provide nonrandom direction to the college. In fact, an intelligent administration would be well advised to anticipate these sorts of dilemmas, so that, by steering a slightly different course, the dilemma can be bypassed. For example, if a bifurcation is anticipated, then posturing only slightly toward the left could suffice to ensure ending up on opinion base x_1 rather than x_2. Thus, even an intelligent administration could benefit from an understanding of models of algorithmic colleges and universities. The models illustrate possible dilemmas that can be avoided by adroit leadership.

Administrative Inertia. This basic assumption may be changed, for example, using either the Maxwell rule or the voting rule (Zeeman, 1977), so that policy is always set at (one of) the highest peak(s) of public opinion. Such a change in assumptions produces a slightly different model, equally suspectible to dynamical terminology and equally fraught with dilemmas (Zeeman, 1980).

Summary and Application

While this chapter has introduced some vocabulary and a few grammar rules of a qualitative mathematical language, it would be a mistake to conclude that this language is merely a presentation of some techniques that institutional researchers can add to their bag of tricks. Elsewhere (Johnson and Lacher, 1981), we have suggested that this approach provides a theoretical framework for all institutional research studies. We believe that topological models are as rigorous as, and often more appropriate than, algebraic structures; that our traditional tests of means are not applicable to all models that underlie our social systems; that the nonlinear world of higher education lends itself to dynamical systems models; that sequential effects are interesting phenomena and should be studied using qualitative mathematical approaches (Hillix, Hershman, and Wicker, 1979); and that the qualitative approach contains the equations needed to bridge the gap between institutional data, which are difficult to measure, and social interactions, which are difficult to compute (Poston and Stewart, 1978).

In practice, if we are to reconcile the data collected at one institution with the data collected at another for purposes of useful exchange, we need either total agreement on the scales to be used, or we need to learn how to state qualitative conclusions. We recommend the latter, because the ability to state qualitative conclusions reveals new possibilities for understanding the influence of the underlying dynamic on how people make up their minds. Our model states that a gradient dynamical system involving parameters of an admissions policy can exhibit characteristics of local maxima and local minima of opinion regarding that policy.

We have defined a system as any phenomenon which can be described by a collection of numerical variables x, y, z, while a dynamical system has been defined as one in which those variables change with time: $x(t)$, $y(t)$, $z(t)$. A basic application problem is to understand, or to discover, precisely how those variables depend on time. In many cases, it is known how the rate of change of each variable depends on the values of all the variables, and, since rate of change is a derivative, it is appropriate to apply differential equations.

We have defined a parameterized dynamical system as an entire collection of these differential equations depending on further variables a, b, c, which are called parameters. We have illustrated the Maxwell rule and the delay rule. Further, stationary bifurcation, hysteresis loop, saddle point, and cusp have been defined, illustrated, and related to possible distributions of opinion, which changes over time. We are now ready to apply this model to an example of how institutional researchers can use this qualitative method of describing a system to communicate new possibilities to other institutional researchers who share a similar problem.

Let us suppose, for example, that all colleges and universities are faced with a new kind of student created by a common social or economic event. The recent case of returning Vietnam War veterans will serve to illustrate how the model can be applied. Initially, admission policy committees assumed that public opinion supported educating veterans who had served their country in an unpopular war, and the admissions policy was relaxed. Lower academic standards seemed justified in order to accommodate those who had defended the flag. The policy committees found, however, that, as the number of admitted veterans grew larger, a second view began to gain support. This second view held that academic standards were being lowered to the point where higher education in general was losing credibility. The admissions policy committee then faced a conflict between support for patriotism and support for academic standards. Our model suggests that either the policy would have been adjusted as soon as the academic standards view gained more support than the patriotism view (Maxwell rule) or the policy committees would wait until the support for patriotism was exhausted to shift suddenly to the policy that had the greatest support at that time (delay rule). If the policy committees behave in the way that most policy makers do, the model predicts that the committees would have applied the delay rule and waited until the last possible moment to switch from a policy supported by patriotism to a policy supported by desire for higher academic standards.

Institutional researchers who were collecting quantitative data for the policy decisions (for example, studies of the predictive value of veterans' SAT scores, analysis of the cost per student credit hour of remedial instruction) were able to exchange experiences with other institutional researchers who had used similar predictive scales to perform instructional cost studies. Chances are that these exchanges yielded an unrewarding result, because, when quantitative conclusions were compared, differences in populations of students, cost-accounting methods, and scales used to measure student performance created problems. Attempts at quantitative data exchange that required agreement on the scales to be used were probably difficult at best and generally inconclusive.

Qualitative conclusions, however, could have been made. We argue that they would have had more value, because they would draw attention to the whole event, not to essentially incompatible parts. In order to make qualitative conclusions, institutional researchers should seek guidance from books like Zeeman's (1977) *Catastrophe Theory*. Such a picture catalogue can be used to identify geometric shapes and to select the one that is most like the qualitative aspects of the whole event. There are many shapes to choose from ranging from the simple geometry of the fold to the complex geometry of the butterfly. Full descriptions of the mathematics of these shapes are included, along with many applications to the natural and social sciences.

Once the qualitative features of possible shapes are understood, then one shape can be selected for a particular situation. In the example of the admission policy on returning veterans, the cusp seems an appropriate shape, since we have two conflicting factors, patriotism and academic standards, that result in support for different levels of a relatively selective or permissive admission policy. The institutional researcher needs to label the parts of the model selected from the catalogue, see if the result makes sense, and then consult others who have worked with the same problem at other institutions. If the model is appropriate for this example, we would expect from the delay rule that any large change in policy would be sudden; we should see a bifurcation of opinion—support for either patriotism or academic standards; we should be able to trace some divergence (two institutions could start close together in their policy but end up far apart, because they lean toward opposite support bases and become trapped by the delay rule); we should be able to see some hysteresis—caused by the delayed change in policy;

40

Figure 3. Cusp Model Applied of Admissions Policy

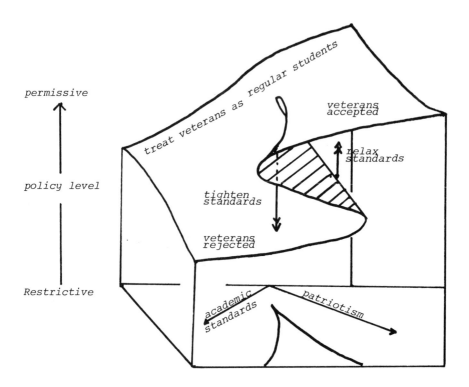

and we should be able to see an inaccessible region, where policy must jump from one extreme to the other, because there is no level of support for a neutral policy.

Once institutional researchers focus upon these qualitative conclusions, they can discuss their different experiences with different pathways and different timing of decisions. As the various qualitative conclusions are compared, it is not necessary to have equal scales in order to reach general conclusions about the relationship of the variables to time, formulate some hypotheses about the rate of change of the variables involved, and apply the appropriate differential equations.

We believe that this approach would provide institutional researchers with a rich basis for discussion and exchange of qualitative information while avoiding the unproductive complications of attempts to reach universal agreement on definitions and scales.

References

Hillix, W. A., and Hershman, R. L., and Wicker, F. S. *Catastrophe Theory in the Behavioral Sciences*. San Diego, Calif.: Navy Personnel Research and Development Center, 1979.

Johnson, F. C., and Lacher, R. C. "Contributions of Nonlinear Dynamical Systems to Decision Making." Paper presented at the European Association for Institutional Research Forum. Louvain la-Nouve, Belgium, 1981.

Poston, T., and Stewart, I. *Catastrophe Theory and Its Application*. London: Pitman, 1978.

Zeeman, E. C. "Catastrophe Models in Administration." In P. Staskey (Ed.), *Meeting the Challenges of the Eighties: Redirection of Resources for Renewal*. Tallahassee, Fla.: Association for Institutional Research, 1980.

Zeeman, E. C. *Catastrophe Theory: Selected Papers 1972–1977*. Reading, Mass.: Addison-Wesley, 1977.

Note: A comprehensive bibliography on catastrophe theory can be obtained from E. C. Zeeman, Mathematics Institute, University of Warwick, Coventry, CV4 7AL, England.

F. Craig Johnson is a professor of Educational Research and past president of the Association for Institutional Research. R. C. Lacher is a professor of mathematics. Both are on the faculty of Florida State University.

A new trend in methods is appearing in both political science and public administration, especially when the results of research are aimed at both practitioners and academics.

Contributions of Political Science and Public Administration to Qualitative Research Methods

Alana Northrop
Kenneth L. Kraemer

Methods in political science have been dominated by a paradigm which assumes that the primary audience is other researchers and scholars and that quantitative measurement, experimental design, and multivariate, parametric statistical analysis are key to the scientific quality and acceptability of research results. In contrast, methods in public administration have been dominated by a paradigm which assumes that qualitative measurement, in-depth open-ended interviewing, and personal observation, which provide depth and richness to research results, are key to substantive validity and to prescriptions that practitioners can use. Yet, as public administration has become a more established field, it, too, has turned to quantitative methods, especially by moving away from

E. Kuhns, S. V. Martorana (Eds.). *New Directions for Institutional Research: Qualitative Methods for Institutional Research*, no. 34. San Francisco: Jossey-Bass, March 1982.

case studies to probability samples. Moreover, a new trend in methods is appearing in both political science and public administration, especially when the results of research are aimed at "pracademics," individuals who are both practitioners and academics. It is now being argued that neither of the two paradigms is intrinsically better than the other. In fact, it is proposed that, when one combines qualitative and quantitative methods, the advantages can offset the disadvantages (Rohner, 1977).

For example, the advantage of sampling as a quantitative method lies in the generalizability of findings. Yet, one disadvantage of probability sampling is the lack of in-depth and detailed understanding of the cases in the sample. Case studies provide such in-depth and detailed understanding, but they are only generalizable to the cases actually studied, not to the population, as in a sample. But, when one combines sampling with case study collection of data, the study gains both generalizable findings and detailed understanding of why the individual cases together suggest certain statistical trends. This is but one example and one argument for mixing qualitative and quantitative methods.

Another attempt to mix the two methods lies in the use of a semistructured field-coded questionnaire. A semistructured field-coded questionnaire mixes the standardization of closed-ended responses with the unstructured interview and investigative techniques of qualitative methods. Another example of mixed methods combines random respondent selection, which reduces bias to measurable error, with purposeful or biased selection of respondents, such as by choosing respondents whom one thinks will be the most knowledgeable in the area under study.

In this chapter, we will discuss the URBIS Project, a four-year study of the management of computing in local government. The project team included both political scientists and public administration scholars. The team designed and implemented a study that used the three ways just described to mix quantitative and qualitative methods. Our aim in this chapter is to explain how we mixed the methods and how our study's conclusions benefited from it.

General Approaches to Mixing Qualitative and Quantitative Methods

The mixing of qualitative and quantitative methods has been referred to as *triangulation*. The term comes from navigation and military strategy. It indicates that different kinds of data have been collected about the same phenomenon (Smith, 1975). There are three kinds of triangulation: between methods, within methods, and holistic (Denzin, 1978).

The between-methods approach is the most common in political science and public administration. Campbell and Fiske (1959) argue that, when more than one method obtains the same conclusion, then we can be more confident that the conclusions are real and not a reflection of the method used. In short, the between-methods approach means that quantitative and qualitative methods are used independently and that the findings are then compared. Thus, it is a check on the external validity of the data.

The within-methods approach uses multiple techniques to collect data within a given method. For instance, within the quantitative method of survey research, one can use multiple scales or variables to tap political ideology. Thus, the within-methods approach is a check for internal consistency in the data.

The holistic approach involves direct mixing of qualitative and quantitative methods. The most common example of this approach is the one that we cited at the beginning of this chapter: combining probability sampling of sites with fieldwork collection of data. Many social scientists (Deising, 1971; Kraemer, Dutton, and Northrop, 1981; McCall and Simmons, 1969; Reiss, 1968; Sieber, 1973; Vidich and Shapiro, 1955) have argued that quantitative methods can make important contributions to fieldwork and that fieldwork can make important contributions to survey research.

In sum, triangulation is not new, although it is just now being more fully appreciated. The URBIS Project used the holistic approach. This is still a rare research method, but it is gaining increasing attention in the fields of political science and public administration.

The Holistic Approach to Mixing Methods

The URBIS research methodology was designed to study computing in organizations in two major phases of research: a census survey of all the larger city and county governments in the United States and a more narrowly focused field analysis of forty-two city governments. In addition, extensive case studies were conducted in various cities and counties to explore and elaborate the research issues and research design. Fuller's elaboration of the research methodology can be found in Hackathorn (1975); Kraemer, Danziger, Dutton, Mood, and Kling (1976); Kraemer, Dutton, and Northrop (1981); and Kraemer and Schetter (1979).

Phase I: Census Survey. The primary intent of the census survey was to provide baseline data on computing arrangements and on policies relating to computing in American local governments. This survey provided a data base from which to analyze characteristic patterns of use and diffusion of current computer technology and also to select appropriate sites for more extensive study in the second phase of the research.

A three-part survey of cities and counties was conducted. One part gathered information on the personal views of the government's chief executive toward computer technology in local government. The second part collected extensive information from each computer installation serving the government, measuring such characteristics of computing as types of equipment, levels and types of personnel and budget, and kinds of policies governing the use of computing. The third part, a questionnaire completed by each computer installation, was an inventory of current and near-future automated applications provided to the local government by the installation.

The criterion for including local governments in the census survey was population size in 1970. The three survey instruments were mailed in early 1975 to all cities with a population of more than 50,000 and to all counties with a population of more than 100,000—403 municipalities and 310 counties in all. The chief executive questionnaire was returned by 82 percent of the cities and 77 percent of the counties. The two computer installation questionnaires were returned by 81 percent of the cities and 67 percent of the counties that used computers (Hackathorn, 1975).

Phase II: Field Studies. The central purpose of the second phase of the project was to perform an empirical evaluation of the impacts of automated information systems on local governments and to specify the effects of alternative management policies in order to identify policies that improve the performance of computer technology. It is this second phase of the study that best illustrates the mixing of methods in the research. Four aspects were involved: design, tasks to study, respondents, and data collection.

Design. The first aspect of our study that mixed quantitative and qualitative methods was the combination of survey research based on probability sampling of cities with field observations. For Phase II, we needed a sample that was small enough to allow intensive field research at each site and large enough to enable us to make generalizations. We decided to study only municipal governments, so that the organizational units would be comparable. Our interest in alternative computing configurations, many of which were relatively rare, meant that we could not use conventional probability sampling, since it would not provide a sample of sites with extreme policy mixes from which the optimal policies for America's future cities could be identified (Kraemer and others, 1976).

Our solution was a variation on disproportionate stratified sampling technique. Six key computer package characteristics were identified: total number of automated applications, degree of centralization of the package, charging policy for computing services, sophistication of hardware, level of integration of data in the system, and extent of user involvement in applications adoption, design, evaluation, and programming. Each of the six variables was dichotomized on the basis of Phase I data for city governments, with all scores below the third quartile treated as low scores and all scores above the third quartile treated as high. This produced a partitioned sample with 2^6 or 64 strata.

All cities were located in their proper stratum on the basis of actual Phase I scores or of estimated scores for cases where there were no data for the variable. A balanced set of forty strata was then selected at random, ensuring that there would be twenty cities on each side of each policy (with two additional strata to compensate for city refusals and missing data). Where a stratum had no cities within it, the city with the closest variable scores was employed. Finally, one city was selected at random from each stratum.

Our research design meant that the field sites would not be fully representative of computing in all cities in Phase I. In general, Phase II cities were more populated, more highly automated, and more sophisticated, decentralized, and integrated in their computing than Phase I cities were. Phase II cities involved users more with the computer package, and they more often charged for computer use (Kraemer, Dutton, and Northrop, 1981). While the municipal governments that we studied in Phase II were somewhat more developed with regard to computing than other municipalities in 1975, we did much of our empirical research in Phase II, as well as in other parts of our research, in governmental settings with more typical computing.

The probability sampling of cities, which formed the basis for our survey research, was combined with field observations in each of the cities selected. Six investigators, including the authors, spent an average of three person-weeks in each of eight sites or more. Team members were responsible for conducting about forty personal interviews in each city, distributing between fifty and a hundred questionnaires, and writing a case study of the visit. Thus, our design provided both survey and fieldwork data on each city.

Tasks to Study. The second aspect of the project that mixed quantitative and qualitative methods was the choice of tasks to study. While most researchers speak generally about the impact of computers and computer-based information systems, we felt that assessment should focus on the individual tasks that computers perform. For example, statements that computers save time are more easily and objectively assessed by studying specific computerized tasks. Thus, we used the term *information-processing task* (IPT) to signify an activity that has a specific objective, that explicitly involves information processing, and that can be automated (Kraemer and others, 1976). For example, most cities regularly issue a payroll. This task requires translating records of hours worked, pay rates, and payroll deductions into a payroll check. Thus, *payroll processing* can be designated an IPT. However, the more than 300 IPTs that can be automated cover the full range of services provided by most city governments (although the IPTs do cluster in functional areas). Therefore, in order to be able to generalize beyond any specific IPT and in order to investigate IPTs in systematic fashion, it was necessary to focus on a small sample of IPTs.

The sampling relied on two criteria. First, we wished to generalize beyond the specific type of activity that a particular IPT involves, so we sampled IPTs from each of six generic types: record keeping, calculating and printing, record searching, record restructuring, sophisticated analytics, and process control. Second, since we could investigate only a few IPTs, we wanted to generalize beyond any single functional area of government services. Hence, we chose seven IPTs within four functional areas: police, courts, finance, and planning and management. Table 1 indicates the general characteristics of each IPT type and the specific IPTs that were studied.

**Table 1. Types of Information-Processing Tasks
and Associated Applications**

Type	Characterization	Applications Chosen
Record Keeping	Activities that primarily involve entry, updating, and storage of data, with a secondary need for access; the computer facilitates manageable storage and easy updating for nearly unlimited amounts of information.	Traffic Ticket Processing
Calculating and Printing	Activities that primarily involve sorting, calculating, and printing stored data to produce specific operational outputs; this type utilizes the computer's capabilities as a high-speed data processor.	Budget Control (Reporting)
Record Searching	Activities where access to and search of data files is of primary importance; by defining parameters, relevant cases can be retrieved from a file with speed and comprehensiveness; the on-line capability of the computer is particular useful.	Detective Investigative Support; Patrol Officer Support
Record Restructuring	Activities that involve reorganization, reaggregation, and analysis of data; the computer is used to link data from diverse sources or to summarize large volumes of data as management and planning information.	Policy Analysis
Sophisticated Analytics	Activities that utilize sophisticated visual, mathematical, simulation, or other analytical methods to examine data; the special capabilities of computers make possible the manipulation of data about complex, interdependent phenomena.	Patrol Manpower Allocation
Process Control	Activities that approximate a cybernetic system; data about the state of a system are continually monitored and fed back to a human or automatic controller that steers the system towards a performance standard; the computer's capabilities for real-time monitoring and direction of activities are utilized.	Budget Control (Monitoring)

Thus, by focusing on seven specific IPTs within six generic types of tasks and four functional areas, we increased our capacity to generalize beyond any particular IPT or functional area and to collect objective indicators of policy outcomes. In sum, our study utilized sampling theory to guide IPT case selection and thereby improve the generalizablity of findings.

Respondents. Respondent selection was the third aspect of the project that mixed quantitative and qualitative methods. The methods used for respondent selection were specifically tailored to each information-processing task. The general strategy was to identify the roles most important in each information-processing task and to sample among people who had those roles. Certain roles, such as mayor, manager, and head of the budget-reporting unit, defined specific respondents. In these cases, every respondent was contacted. For other roles, such as council member, detective, and traffic ticket clerk, there were larger groups of potential respondents. In these cases, we tried to approximate a random sample of these respondents at every site. Thus, respondents were selected both randomly and purposefully.

For example, one of the IPTs that we studied was patrol officer support. Interviews were conducted with members of the police force who were thought to be most knowledgeable about the automation of police information used by patrol officers: the police chief, two patrol lieutenants, and the officer responsible for computer implementation. In addition, ten patrol officers were selected at random to complete a questionnaire about their assessment of the usefulness of automated information.

Data Collection. The fourth aspect of the project that mixed quantitative and qualitative methods was the use of semistructured field-coded questionnaires along with self-administered questionnaires. Self-administered questionnaires were completed by between fifty and a hundred users of computing in each city. This lengthy questionnaire measured users' perceptions of the impacts, problems, and benefits associated with computing. Self-administered questionnaires were also completed by the data processing managers and staff of each computer installation in each city.

In addition, about forty personal interviews were conducted with elected officials and municipal personnel involved with the seven IPTs studied in each city. These interviews were semi-structured and field coded. That is, fieldworkers used cross-examination, department records, their own judgment, and a general investigative approach in order to code each city on the basis of a structured set of items. For example, an investigator might speak with a police chief, several police captains and lieutenants, detectives, and the city manager as well as search police documents in order to determine who were minor and major participants in decisions about the adoption of computer applications to support detective investigation activities. We refer to this strategy as *structured field coding* in order to indicate its central feature: Cities are coded in a structured way, but the coding is done in the field, not on the basis of schemes developed to combine various sources and items of data long after the investigator has left the city. We refer to this strategy as *semistructured* in that each field-worker was allowed to emphasize the data source that, from his fieldwork experience, seemed the most applicable and trustworthy. The field coding was structured by a questionnaire developed and pretested for each of the six IPTs.

In sum, the URBIS project combined quantitative and qualitative methods in four different ways: survey research in cities based on probability sampling, with fieldwork collection of data; sampling theory to guide IPT case selection; random and purposeful respondent selection; and semistructured field-coded questionnaires. This holistic approach to data collection proved beneficial to our study in several ways.

The Benefits of Mixing Methods

One of the greatest benefits from the holistic approach is a person in the field was available to investigate further and explain conflicting survey information as it was collected so there was no time gap and less puzzling and inaccurate data. When one is collecting opinion data, there is always the possibility that experience differs from perception. Our aim was to study the actual experience that cities had with automation. Consequently, the fieldworker served to bridge the gap between perception and experience.

Another benefit that stems from the combination of fieldwork with survey research is evident when one is back from the field, poring over correlation coefficients. One of our IPTs was patrol officer allocation. Quantitative data indicated that automating the way in which a police department allocates officers throughout the city does not increase the efficiency and rationality of allocation over manual allocation of officers. Yet, in the other five IPTs, automation always improved performance. Of course, patrol officer allocation was the only IPT that fit the generic type of information processing called *sophisticated analytics*. This being the case, our policy advice would be unique for this IPT; that is, we would suggest that the costs of automation are in no way balanced by the benefits. However, our fieldwork experience told us that this recommendation was totally unsubstantiated, because no police department really used its automated patrol allocation program. Some cities obtained the program but never used it. Other cities used the program but ignored its results and, instead, used their own experience to allocate officers. In short, without our fieldwork collection of data, we would have recommended a policy that would be costly to police departments and the citizens they serve.

Finally, the quality of any study is judged by its audience. The intended audience of the URBIS Project was both other academics and practitioners. Practitioners are suspicious of academics who portend to know more than the people who really do the work. But, because we did case studies, we were able to recount actual experiences of cities that gave context and texture to our survey data, and we thereby improved the usefulness and acceptability of our study's policy recommendations. Our survey design also allowed us to address what would be normal concerns of other researchers and academics about generalizability. Although our method of sampling cities was unconventional, we were able to define precisely how well our sample described the population of cities, because we had precise information on how the sample differed from the population of cities. Moreover, the usual problems of generalization from small samples were overcome, because our design strategy was aimed at identifying policies found to be successful in advanced cities that less-advanced cities might usefully emulate. Thus, we were not trying to make descriptive statements about all cities. Rather, we sought to make prescriptive policy statements for all cities based upon our study of the experience of the most advanced cities.

Conclusion

A research project as extensive as the URBIS Project provides many types of data and facilitates consideration of the research issues from many perspectives. Since most empirical methods and measures are subject to one or another form of bias, it is usually desirable to employ alternative methods and measures that attempt to tap the same phenomenon (Webb and others, 1966). In analyzing the computing in larger American local governments, we used numerous exploratory case studies; an extensive, multipart survey instrument in virtually the entire population of cities and counties; and intensive field research in a relatively large number of sites, where structured case coding, discursive case reports, and a widely distributed survey instrument were used.

Our experience with this holistic approach to mixing quantitative and qualitative methods has convinced us that it deserves attention in political science and public administration research and from social scientists generally. While the problem of data replication may never be solved when one employs qualitative methods, the mixing of quantitative and qualitative methods does allow for statistical analysis and secondary analysis of data, which a qualitative study alone does not. And, we have found that the value of qualitative and quantitative methods combined is both positive and major, especially when the results of research are aimed at multiple audiences.

References

Campbell, D. T., and Fiske, D. W. "Convergent and Discriminant Validation by the Multitract-Multimethod Matrix." *Psychological Bulletin*, 1959, *56*, 81–105.

Deising, P. *Patterns of Discovery in the Social Sciences*. Chicago: Aldine-Atherton, 1971.

Denzin, N. K. *The Research Act*. New York: McGraw-Hill, 1978.

Hackathorn, L. *The URBIS Census Survey*. Irvine: Public Policy Research Organization, University of California, 1975.

Kraemer, K. L., Danziger, J. N., Dutton, W. H., Mood, A. M., and Kling, R. "A Future Cities Research Design for Policy Analysis," *Socioeconomic Planning Sciences*, 1976, *10* (5), 199–211.

Kraemer, K. L., Dutton, W. H., and Northrop, A. *The Management of Information Systems*. New York: Columbia University Press, 1981.

Kraemer, K. L., and Schetter, D. *The URBIS Project: Administrative Summary*. Irvine: Public Policy Research Organization, University of California, 1979.

McCall, G. J., and Simmons, J. L. *Issues in Participant Observation: A Test and Reader*. Reading, Mass.: Addison-Wesley, 1969.

Reiss, A. T. "Stuff and Nonsense About Social Surveys and Observation." In H. Becker, B. Geer, D. Reisman, and R. Weiss (Eds.), *Institutions and the Person*. Chicago: Aldine, 1968.

Rohner, R. P. "Advantages of the Comparative Method of Anthropology." *Behavior Science Research*, 1977, *12*, 117–144.

Sieber, S. D. "The Integration of Fieldwork and Survey Methods." *American Journal of Sociology*, 1973, *78*, 1335–1359.

Smith, H. W. *Strategies of Social Research: The Methodological Imagination*. Englewood Cliffs, N.J.: Prentice-Hall, 1975.

Spindler, G. E. (Ed.). *Being an Anthropologist*. New York: Holt, Rinehart and Winston, 1970.

Vidich, A. J., and Shapiro, G. "A Comparison of Participant Observation and Survey Data." *American Sociological Review*, 1955, *20*, 28–33.

Webb, E. J., Campbell, D. T., Schwartz, R. D., and Sechrest, L. *Unobtrusive Measures: Nonreactive Research in the Social Sciences*. Chicago: Rand McNally, 1966.

Alana Northrop teaches American politics and quantitative methods at California State University, Fullerton, and she is an associate research political scientist at the Public Policy Research Organization at the University of California, Irvine.

Kenneth L. Kraemer is a professor of management in the Graduate School of Management and director of the Public Policy Research Organization at the University of California, Irvine.

*History is not what happened but what
human beings do to acquire reliable knowledge
about what happened and how they convert
such knowledge into an enlarged and enriched
understanding of reality and their place
in the world.*

History and Qualitative Methodology

Mark H. Curtis

This chapter is not a report on research or a critical review of recent research. It is an essay, a distillation of experience. It is reflective in that it draws on a career of scholarship, teaching, and academic administration for ideas and principles. It is speculative in so far as it suggests that certain features of historical study can make contributions to qualitative methodology.

Two historian philosophers with very different positions have had special influence on my view of history. They are Carl L. Becker and R. G. Collingwood. Among their works that I consider particularly useful are Becker's "Detachment and the Writing of History" (1910) and *Everyman His Own Historian: Essays on History and Politics* (1936) and Collingwood's *The Idea of History* (1956). Other works of special value are G. R. Elton's *The Practice of History* (1967), J. H. Hexter's *Reappraisals in History* (1961), and Trygve R. Tholfsen's *Historical Thinking: An Introduction* (1967).

A Word on History

History, as I understand it, is an intellectual effort to make sense of past human experience. It is not, despite common usage,

E. Kuhns, S. V. Martorana (Eds.). *New Directions for Institutional Research: Qualitative Methods for Institutional Research*, no. 34. San Francisco: Jossey-Bass, March 1982.

the past itself. The past is the object of historical inquiry, but it is not history. The past has left evidence of what has been thought, said, and done, but it has not left such evidence in forms that are self-explanatory or that reveal self-evident connections—either functional or intellectual—among thoughts, words, and deeds. Hence, to understand the past in its complexity, with its consistencies and inconsistencies, its continuities and discontinuities, its seeming certainties and its obvious ambiguities, requires an intellectual effort that, first of all, seeks for all available evidence of what has been thought, said, and done; then, considers critically the significance that each piece of evidence has in its context; and finally, undertakes to make intelligible the changes that have occurred in thoughts, words, and deeds in the course of time. In short, history is not what happened but what human beings do to acquire reliable knowledge about what happened and how they convert such knowledge into an enlarged and enriched understanding of reality and their place in the world. Such understanding is part of what it means to be well informed. It can be used to evaluate situations and to make decisions about the promise or peril of alternative courses of action.

One of the things that this definition of history takes for granted is that the historian is caught up in the process, or at least in the end of the process, that he or she is trying to understand. This existential plight of the historian needs to be examined, because critics can use it to dismiss the validity of historical knowledge.

The fact that the historian is a part of unfolding human experience calls for awareness of possible pitfalls, but it does not make historical study invalid. In studying the remote past, an investigator may run afoul of anachronism and interpret evidence in terms of the present, not its own context. In examining recent developments, the historian may introduce personal feelings and attitudes to distort the meaning of the evidence. In both cases, the antidote is a compound of disinterestedness and sensitivity to context. Disinterestedness, an achievable goal as contrasted to objectivity, is a product of thorough study joined with self-knowledge and imagination. It means recognizing that others are also immersed, but in different circumstances, in the process of experience and then self-consciously thinking one's way into their situation. Sensitivity to context brings a means of checking the validity of an historian's perceptions and interpretations. Taken together, disinterestedness and sensitivity to context can establish reliability in one's findings.

The concept of context is another major assumption of historical study. As I use the term, *context* has two separable but interrelated meanings. I suspect that the first of these is generally shared by all concerned with qualitative research. It predicates that any thought or act is part of a web of experience and, indeed, is a function of that web. To assert this point is not to maintain that all thinkers or actors are fully aware of the web of experience in which they live, think, and act. Probably very few are, and even fewer are likely to have reflected enough on their situation to develop a self-conscious, sophisticated understanding of it. Most individuals and the groups of which they are part seem content to appropriate enough of their web of experience to supply a modus vivendi that incorporates pragmatically all that they have consciously or unconsciously perceived to be vital to their existence, if not their well-being. The web of experience itself, to which the modus vivendi can be a clue, is, however, the matter of basic significance to the historian.

Context, as already mentioned, has a second meaning or characteristic that seems to lie at the root of the contribution that history can make to qualitative research. In the mind of this historian, at least, the first meaning of context truncates the concept. The second meaning is, therefore, not merely interrelated with the first but an essential element of the whole. Briefly, the past is part of the context of the present. What has been thought, said, and done is the ground of what is being thought, said, and done. Therefore, to comprehend in its fullness what is requires an understanding of what was. This point does not rest merely on the idea of continuity, important as that is, but recognizes that the immediate past has a significant effect on the present by setting conditions, such as resources, issues, judgments of situations, motivations, sense of unsatisfied needs, and perceptions of possibilities, that thinkers and actors in the present have available for their life and activities.

Uses of History in Qualitative Research

The Starting Point for Qualitative Analysis. Patton (1980) has defined the focus of qualitative research in these terms: "Researchers using qualitative methods strive to understand phenomena and situations as a whole; evaluators using qualitative methods attempt to understand programs as wholes. . . . In contrast to experimental designs, which manipulate and measure relationships among a few carefully selected and narrowly defined variables, the holistic approach to research design is open to gathering data on any number of aspects of the setting under study in order to put together a complete picture of the social dynamic of a particular situation or program. This means that . . . each case, event, or setting being studied is treated as a unique entity with its own particular meaning and constellation of relationships emerging from and related to the context within which it exists" (Patton, 1980, p. 40). If what has been asserted about the nature of historical study has any validity, then a notion of history in which context has critical importance may make important contributions to the methodology of qualitative research.

The first contribution that history can make lies in establishing the starting point for qualitative analysis. What was the actual situation at the moment that the program or project being evaluated got under way? What conditions evoked a sense of need for change? Who were the persons most concerned about the need for change? How well had they analyzed the situation, and how clearly had they conceived the objectives of the project? Was there general agreement about the need for change and about the objectives? If there was substantial divergence of opinion about either, how did the initiators of the project win support for their proposals? All these questions are ones that historical study can address. Indeed, they are the kind of questions that an historian is trained to ask in order to establish the full context of the situation under investigation.

Control for Qualitative Research. Because, as Patton (1980, p. 40) notes, qualitative research studies cases or events that are "unique" in the sense that each has "its own particular meaning and constellation of relationships," methods for controlling or setting the basis for evaluation differ from methods used in quantitative research. If each situation is unique in its own setting and context, it cannot be replicated in its original state in another setting or context to provide a control or comparison case. Even the very best simulation on the most sophisticated computer will not do. Controls for qualitative research would seem, therefore, to require methods of a very different order. They demand such things, for instance, as comparison of what has come to be with what was and the sophisticated contrast of differential development in cases similar to the case under study.

Again, I suggest that history can be helpful in the question of controls for qualitative research. The lines of inquiry required are the life and breath of historical scholarship. The very essence of history is the study of change through time. Although the normal scale of historical research is usually generations and centuries, it can and does include change within short spans of time. The methods in determining the changes that have in fact occurred and the significance that should be assigned them are the same in both cases.

A word of caution is in order. When working within the scale of generations and centuries, the historian can be more certain of the final consequences of change than when examining a case whose developments are still in process. Yet, the historical scholar can bring to the latter case possibilities for judgment and evaluation that deserve attention. The historian's knowledge of the factors or configurations of experience that in other situations have determined the acceptance or rejection of change can be valuable in evaluating the significance of what is happening as events unfold.

Comparative study, which is also a well established field of historical scholarship, may also be useful to qualitative research. Historians have long engaged in the investigation of the similarities and differences between historical phenomena, such as revolutions and reform movements. They have also examined why an institution that appears at approximately the same time in two or more societies develops in significantly different ways. Although these examples may seem remote from the problems of qualitative evaluation of limited situations, I believe that they are relevant. Again, methods and lines of inquiry developed to pursue large-scale studies are, I am convinced, applicable to studies of lesser scope. What characteristics of two situations make it possible to compare developments within them? Do the differences between two cases assist an investigator in understanding the nature of the process under study? Within different configurations of conditions and circumstances, are there factors that seem to have similar consequences, although the consequences differ in degree? What effect does the sequence in which developments occur seem to have on their outcomes? These and other questions that historians have asked in pursuing comparative studies may have some place in qualitative research.

Summary and Conclusion

Some readers may have expected a detailed explanation of historical methods and how they are applicable to qualitative research. Eventually, such a how-to disquisition would be useful, but I believe that it is more important at this stage in the development of qualitative research to heighten awareness of the contributions that history can make to qualitative studies than to spell out the operational steps by which the methodology of history can be applied.

In 1977 and 1978, I directed Project Athena, which evaluated the impact of the Institutional Grants Program of the National Endowment for the Humanities. My colleagues and I discovered that history was essential for our work. As I reflect on that experience, two occasions on which we used historical research stand out sharply in my memory.

In evaluating the impact of institutional grants, we had two major questions to answer: First, how had institutional grants served national interests; second, how had institutional grants met the needs of the colleges and universities that had received them? In each case, historical research was indispensable. To establish the national interests that the grants were intended to serve, we used historical research to analyze the act of Congress authorizing the National Endowment for the Humanities, debates in Congress during the passage of that act, intra-agency memoranda, minutes of the National Council of the Humanities, budget requests submitted both to the Office of Management and Budget and to Congress, and personal interviews with former officers of the Endowment. This research not only gave us a firm understanding of the national goals at the outset of the Institutional Grants Program but also revealed how and when those goals had changed during the seven-year period under evaluation. Likewise, in evaluating the impact of grants on the programs of colleges and universities, we discovered that historical investigations were valuable in checking an institution's perceptions of what was needed and what had occurred against what the full context of the situation disclosed.

The history of historical studies seem to provide the best clue to why history is important for qualitative research. From the days of Herodotus to the present, those who have tried to limit historical studies to past politics have found it impossible to do so. Time and again, historians have discovered that, even to understand the political events of the past, they have had to expand their inquiries little by little to encompass the context in which the political events have unfolded. The Declaration of Independence is an act passed by representatives of the English colonies of North America, assembled in what they called a Continental Congress. Yet, to understand what that act meant, as Garry Wills (1979) recently has shown, requires an intensive study not just of the records of the Continental Congress and an analysis of the document written to justify it but of a long train of events and the attitudes, philosophical and moral ideas, and ways of life of the men who passed it. What this illustration means for qualitative research is that historians can make valuable contributions to it because their professional outlook and training predispose them to examine events in their whole context. Historians operate on the assumption that the events and situations that they study cannot be replicated. The past does not repeat itself. Hence, the process of knowing and understanding the past is an intellectual effort that recovers the past through thorough exploration of evidence, critical thought, and imagination.

In conclusion, therefore, I submit that history and the professional perspectives and lines of inquiry of historians are vital to qualitative research. If all investigators concerned with qualitative studies cannot also be historians, they should ally themselves with an historian as either a coinvestigator or a constant advisor.

References

Becker, C. L. "Detachment and the Writing of History." *Atlantic Monthly*, 1910, *106*, 524–536.

Becker, C. L. *Everyman His Own Historian: Essays on History and Politics.* New York: Crofts, 1936.

Collingwood, R. G. *The Idea of History.* New York: Galaxy Books, 1956.

Elton, G. R. *The Practice of History.* New York: Crowell, 1967.

Hexter, J. H. *Reappraisals in History.* New York: Harper & Row, 1961.

Patton, M. Q. *Qualitative Evaluation Methods.* Beverly Hills, Calif.: Sage, 1980.

Tholfsen, T. R. *Historical Thinking: An Introduction.* New York: Harper & Row, 1967.

Wills, G. *Inventing America: Jefferson's Declaration of Independence.* New York: Random House, 1979.

Mark H. Curtis is president of the Association of American Colleges. Educated as an historian, he was president of Scripps, one of the Claremont Colleges. In 1977–1978, he was director of Project Athena, an evaluation of the impact of the Institutional Grants Program of the National Endowment for the Humanities.

*Naturalistic inquiry on students can follow the
flow through stages of pre-entry, entry, intervening experience, and exit, as well as being concerned with outcomes.*

Improving Institutional
Decisions Through
Qualitative Research
on Students

Richard L. Alfred

The continuing pressure experienced by college and university
faculty and administrators from declining resources has led to a
condition in which students are a neglected dimension in postsecondary education research. The recency of professional research
on student development, combined with the decline in resources,
has forced faculty and administrators to shift the emphasis of
research to quantitative measurement. In the quantitative model,
students are viewed as a generator of resources, not as a locus for
research on educational development. Improvement in student
flow is a requisite for improvement in the operating budget. Given
current problems of resource development and allocation, postsecondary institutions have no choice but to view quantitative
research as the wave of the future until economic conditions dictate
a change.

E. Kuhns, S. V. Martorana (Eds.). *New Directions for Institutional Research: Qualitative
Methods for Institutional Research*, no. 34. San Francisco: Jossey-Bass, March 1982.

Research on student flow is quantitative research in the best sense of the term. Research variables are specified in explicit relationships, and a linear relationship is assumed between level of resources and improvement or decline in measures of student flow: headcount enrollment, course and program attrition, projections of future enrollment, graduation rates, and student outcomes in the world of work and further education. Quantitative research on students is essential if institutions are to respond to the needs of state legislatures, coordinating boards, and local, state, and federal agencies for information about the cost benefits of education. It is not sufficient, however, to explain the impact of college on students or to provide a comprehensive data base for decisions about students. The need exists to expand earlier work on student development, to consider new questions, and to extend research into new areas of inquiry if faculty and administrators are to make informed decisions about students. Informed decisions require qualitative data—detailed and descriptive data about the situations, interactions, and observed behavior of students at the program and institutional levels. Faculty and administrators engaged in decision making that affects students can use data of this type to identify the desirable outcomes of college attendance, to develop programs and services necessary to improve student outcomes, and to evaluate the quality of these outcomes as they relate to specific programs and services. Qualitative data are a vehicle for improvement of institutional decisions at various stages of interaction between students and the college environment.

The focus of this chapter is on the role of qualitative research as a vehicle for improvement of decisions about students. The chapter examines the types of decisions that can and should be addressed through qualitative research, the objectives and methods of research, and the application of qualitative research data to decisions about students. It also considers the utility of qualitative research when applied to programmatic decisions involving students and the benefits of such research for the larger social setting.

Time, Training, and Resources

Ideally, qualitative research is aimed at understanding the characteristics, needs, development modes, and outcomes experienced by students in relationship to the college environment. The strategy of research is to allow important dimensions of the individual-group-environment relationship to emerge from analysis of student behavior and attitudes without supposing in advance what those dimensions will be. The qualitative methodologist attempts to understand the multiple interrelationships among dimensions that emerge from student data without making prior assumptions about the linear relationships among narrowly defined, organizational variables (Patton, 1980). In short, qualitative research on students means that an understanding of student needs, characteristics, development modes, and outcomes emerges from experience with students. The approach to research is inductive. The qualitative researcher gathers data on any number of aspects of the students under study in order to construct a complete picture of the student-environment relationship.

Qualitative research on students of the form just described is neither practical nor possible. Colleges and universities do not possess the human and financial resources necessary to undertake a comprehensive research program of this type. Faculty and professional staff assigned responsibility for collection and analysis of research data—data about students obtained through techniques of personal observation, in-depth interviews, open-ended survey questions, and analysis of descriptive statements—require time and training in order to conduct research. Time and training translate into financial resources that are not presently available in institutions undergoing reduction. Faculty and staff cannot commit large blocks of time to research when faced with the competing functions of teaching, advising, committee assignments, and professional service that already command a significant portion of their time.

It is possible for institutions to adopt a modified approach to qualitative research on students. The modified approach would involve careful delimitation of the objectives of research; identification of the situations, events, interactions, and behaviors experienced by students on which the research will focus; and specification of the decision areas that are to be addressed through qualitative research. The advantage of this modified approach is that it provides direction and purpose to the research effort while ensuring efficient use of staff. The disadvantage is that the modified approach can focus too sharply on specific facets of the student phenomena under study, thereby removing unique elements of student behavior and attitudes from the field of observation. Different approaches are appropriate for different situations. The goal of the modified approach is to incorporate the standardized framework characteristic of quantitative measurement with the holistic orientation of the qualitative method. The process of data collection, then, becomes a directed but integrative process involving a unique blend of research objectives, methods, and institutional decisions.

A Model for Research

A model for the modified approach to qualitative research is presented in Figure 1. In this model, three stages of student interaction with the college environment are proposed: entry, intervening, and exit stages (Alfred, 1974). A series of questions can be asked at each stage to determine the focus of research for decisions about students:

Entry Stage

- What are the background characteristics of students? What role do these characteristics play in shaping the fit between students and institutions?
- Do certain types of characteristics predispose certain categories of students to unique patterns of change as part of the college experience?

Intervening Stage

- In what ways do college programs and services account for qualitative change in student behavior and attitudes?
- What evidence is available to document student development in the education, social, and career realms during college attendance?
- What is the impact of college on students, and what factors internal and external to the college environment contribute to this impact?

Exit Stage

- What outcomes in the social, educational, and career realms do students experience following college attendance?
- What perceptions do students have of the college experience after they leave college?

Figure 1. A Model for Research

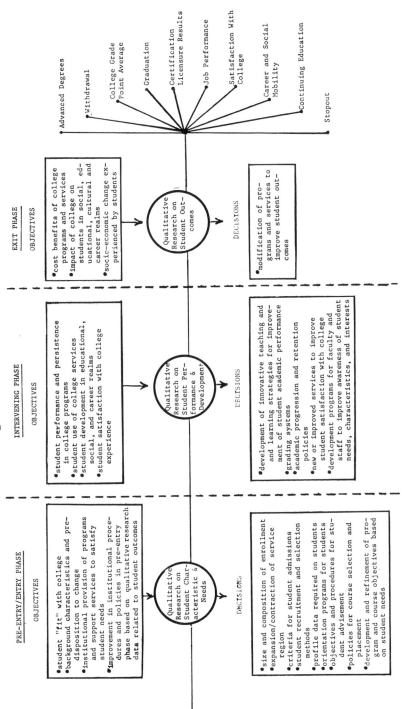

- Did the college experience make a difference in the outlook of students? What was the nature and direction of this difference?

Using these questions as a framework for research, objectives can be developed and qualitative research on students can be conducted in a prescribed format. The goal of research is to obtain detailed data about students at each stage of interaction with the college environment to improve institutional decisions. The types of decisions are multiple, ranging from criteria for the admission of students to modalities for modification of programs and services to improve student outcomes. A variety of research methods are possible at each stage: in-depth interviews with students; analysis of student diaries and portfolios that reflect student experience and interaction with the college environment; descriptions of events, people, situations and interactions; direct quotations about the college experience; review of documents to obtain data about background characteristics of academic performance; open-ended survey questions to determine students' assessment of institutional programs, services, staff, and facilities; in-depth interviews with faculty and staff to obtain detailed descriptions of student behavior; and inferences about student attitudes and opinions based on direct observation of situations, events, interactions, and behaviors.

These methods, in various combinations, provide a comprehensive data base for decisions about students. The linkage between research objectives, methods, and decisions can be described for each stage in the model.

Entry Stage. The objective of research here is to determine the fit between students and the college environment, the predisposition of students to change as a function of background characteristics, and the types of programs and services needed to improve student performance in the college environment. A combination of research methods can be used to generate data about students at entry to college. Closed-ended surveys and diagnostic tests can be used to identify the skills, aptitudes, and background characteristics of incoming students. In-depth interviews can be conducted with students to determine individual needs, interests, and educational and career goals. Meetings with family members and peers can be arranged to gauge the influence of significant others on students' college attendance plans and performance. Such research will yield data on student characteristics, aptitudes, needs, interests, and background experiences that can be used to make decisions about the programs and services that need to be offered to incoming students to improve student-environment relationships. For example, what size and composition of the entering class provides the most opportunities for student growth and development? Should the service region of the college be expanded to achieve the desired quota and mix of students? In what ways can student recruitment and selection methods be changed to reduce the disparity between entering student expectations and environmental conditions? What changes can be made in institutional polices for course selection and placement to improve student performance in programs and courses during the first semester of study? These and other decisions related to student flow and performance can be addressed through qualitative research.

Intervening Stage. The objective of research here is to measure student performance and persistence in college programs and student development in the educational, social, and career realms. Data collected through in-depth interviews with students; observations of student behavior in situations, events, and interactions; review of institutional records; and interviews with campus contacts can be used to improve decisions about students in important areas of activity. For example, what changes in teaching and learning strategies can improve student academic performance? Are academic progression and retention policies clear to students, and do they promote or constrain student development? What types of staff development programs are necessary to improve faculty and staff sensitivity to student needs? Should institutional support services, such as counseling, placement, and tutorial assistance, change in definable ways to improve student academic performance? Are adjustments required in institutional programs and services to improve student retention? What kinds of support services are necessary to provide maximum opportunities for student growth and development during college? Qualitative data on student performance and development can become a source of direction for institutional decisions regarding the allocation of resources to programs and services.

Exit Stage. The objective of research here is to determine the cost benefits of programs and services experienced by students; the impact of college on students in the educational, career, and social realms; and socioeconomic change occurring in students as a result of college attendance. A combination of techniques can be used to identify career patterns and provide evidence of social and economic mobility. In-depth interviews can be conducted with graduates to identify elements of satisfaction or dissatisfaction with the college experience, and open-ended surveys can be used with family members, friends, employers, and fellow workers to determine the modes of personal development that can be attributed to college programs. Data gathered by these methods can be applied to program and resource decisions. For example, what programs do graduating students perceive as important for social and career development? What are the outcomes of college attendance? Do these outcomes match students' educational and career goals? How can college programs and services be modified to improve student outcomes? What adjustments should be made in the allocation of resources to improve student outcomes? Are resources required for new programs? Should existing programs be discontinued in favor of new programs that have promising cost benefits for students? The effect of research at this stage is to improve the quality of decisions through expansion of the data base used to allocate resources to programs and services.

Centrality and Benefits

It is clear that policy makers are disturbed by the unfocused and disorganized way in which colleges and universities confront present exigencies and by their failure to plan for the future. Institutions are supposed to undertake needed research, yet the instances are rare of effective qualitative research on students for use in decisions about long-range plans, allocation of resources to educational programs and services, development of institutional goals, redefinition of missions, and establishment of parameters for institutional development.

Qualitative research on students should be central to the decision-making process. It should provide answers to key questions asked by policy makers at the institutional and extrainstitutional levels. What types of students are attending college now, compared to those who attended college in the recent past? How are these students distributed among programs and courses? How many students drop out or withdraw from college and for what reasons? What types of students drop out, and where do they go? How do institutional programs and services affect student persistence and performance in college? How well do students perform on the job, in the community, in relationships with other people? How responsive, durable, and successful are curricular and budget decisions based on qualitative information about students?

Enabling faculty and administrators to weigh and sift the evidence for various development alternatives, qualitative research on students is a critical ingredient in shaping the future of an institution. An institutional data vacuum invites external intervention and domination either through an imposed plan or through ad hoc decisions. A well-thought out research design based on realistic assessment of an institution's impact on its students invites external support and cooperation, not control. Colleges and universities should know more about their students than external agencies do. Qualitative research provides one method for collecting this information and ensures the continuing progress of colleges and universities toward achieving their stated mission and goals.

References

Alfred, R. L. *Impacts of the Community and Junior College on Students.* Iowa City, Iowa: American College Testing Program and ERIC Clearinghouse for Junior Colleges, 1974.

Patton, M. Q. *Qualitative Evaluation Methods.* Beverly Hills, Calif.: Sage, 1980.

Richard L. Alfred is an associate professor of higher education and director of the Community College Program at the University of Michigan. He has "deep roots" in institutional research in community college districts in Kansas City, Cleveland, and New York.

Qualitative research offers the academic decision maker a rich array of benefits. The unfortunate reality is that institutional researchers are not inclined to use it.

Qualitative Research in Academic Decision Making

Arthur Levine

Over the years, I have visited quite a few colleges. The problems, proposals, and programs that I looked at have varied considerably, but the decisions that needed to be made about them have remained remarkably constant—whether to start something new or end something old, whether to improve or, more recently, retrench an ongoing program. Information is essential for each and every one of these decisions, and qualitative research is an important way of gathering that information.

Qualitative research methods have played an instrumental role in a long list of academic decisions that have made news in the profession in recent years. Examples include the decision to eliminate a number of doctoral degree programs in public and private universities in New York state as recommended by the Board of Regents, a similar decision for doctoral-level programs offered by the state universities in Louisiana, and the decision of the University of Pennsylvania to abolish its School of Nursing.

Persons knowledgeable about how such decisions are made know that they flow not only from quantitative data but also from a "pool of wisdom" filled by information from in-depth inquiry

E. Kuhns, S. V. Martorana (Eds.). *New Directions for Institutional Research: Qualitative Methods for Institutional Research*, no. 34. San Francisco: Jossey-Bass, March 1982.

into the impact of contemplated changes. Information is gathered from students, alumni, faculty, administrators, and so on. In this chapter, I describe one such inquiry from my own experience. This example of short-term qualitative research illustrates the methodology well, although it does not suffice to indicate the design complexity of long-term studies like those just noted.

Short-Term Qualitative Research: An Example

Some years ago, I was studying the different grading systems in use around the country. At the time, many colleges and universities were adding pass-fail grades, usually to supplement letter or numerical grades but occasionally to replace them. Other schools were considering such a change. The critical factor in deciding to adopt the innovation or to retain it was in some cases student pressure or the low esteem accorded grades in the 1960s. But often the decision turned on the question of how pass-fail grading and its various permutations worked. In short, decision makers wanted to know not the philosophic arguments for and against pass-fail grading but how it performed in practice. I set out to collect this information.

I studied pass-fail grading at a number of institutions. One college was chosen because its grading system had been praised both in a national news weekly and in a major daily. I called the school to inquire about its grading system, which combined letter grades with optional pass-fail and written evaluations. Students and faculty both had the option of declaring a course pass-fail. Otherwise, it was letter graded. Students could take as many courses as they wished without grades. College administrators were pleased with the grading system, then nearly two years old. Surveys indicated that faculty and students were by and large satisfied, too. Institutional research showed that a small percentage of students were taking all of their courses pass-fail. Most were taking some of their courses pass-fail. Relatively few undergraduates were opting for only letter grades. This was the anticipated pattern of use. I decided to visit the college to learn firsthand why its new grading system was so successful.

Document Study. I spent two days on campus, working alone. I wanted first to know how the program came into being. I read the minutes of faculty meetings and accounts in student newspapers. I spoke with the principals identified in my readings. The story was this. The grading system had been adopted as the result of enormous student pressure. The specific system approved was a compromise, satisfying neither the reformers nor those who had opposed the initiative. This is not a particularly promising way to begin a new program.

Next, I went to the registrar's office to examine some of the written evaluations and to inquire about the administration of the grading system. I selected a number of student folders, maybe fifty, and proceeded to read through the evaluations until I had a sense of what they were like. I did not need to read them all. The evaluations varied enormously in quality. A small number were excellent—two pages of single-spaced, detailed commentary. A few were abominable—"if I were giving this student a grade, I would give him a B- or 82." Many of the evaluations seemed overly polite, vague, mechanical, or simply uninformative. I could not figure out how a student, a graduate school, or an employer could use them.

Interviewing. I spoke with the registrar. He had opposed the plan, had not changed his mind, and was not doing anything to help. He complained about the cost. Evaluations took up a lot more space than grades. There was one sheet of paper for every course, not one sheet of paper for four years of courses. He estimated that nearly four times as much paper would have to be filed and stored. Moreover, the cost of duplicating the evaluations for graduate schools and employers was steep. Being somewhat short of funds, the registrar handled the transcript problem by ignoring the evaluations. They were not sent out with a student's records. If and when an undergraduate learned about this and requested the evaluations, the student was told to duplicate them himself. In short, there were serious problems both in the quality of the evaluations and in the administration of the program.

Next, I talked with students. I spent an afternoon at a place frequented by commuter students and an evening knocking on dormitory doors. I spoke with students individually and in groups, asking how they used the grading system and what they thought about it. Students were indeed satisfied, but few seemed interested in the written evaluations, so their quality was by and large a matter of only minor concern. In fact, a number of students said that they had not bothered to look at their evaluations, which were available only on request. The result was that, for these undergraduates, the new grading system inaugurated to increase information about course performance provided less information than the letter grades that they automatically received.

As for the pass-fail option, a sizable group of students said that they worked less in such courses. In fact, pass-fail was described as a good way to increase one's grade point average. That is, students described themselves as working hard in the graded courses and slacking off in the nongraded courses. If a student had a four-course load, taking one course pass-fail enabled him to spend a good deal more time grinding away in the three graded courses.

Students also said that they took pass-fail courses almost exclusively outside their majors. This meant that they worked hard on their areas of concentration and reduced their efforts on other subjects. The net result was an increase in students' emphasis on specialization and a decrease in their efforts in general education. In this fashion, the new grading system actually changed the character of the college's curriculum. Moreover, it did so in a manner inconsistent with stated institutional goals.

Finally, students described how the grading system could be manipulated to hike their grades artificially. It was possible to take a test or two before deciding whether to work for a grade or for a pass. High scores on the tests called for letter grades; low scores resulted in a pass.

In sum, the students' conversation convinced me that the new grading system brought with it a fair number of unintended consequences, and a good many of these consequences appeared undesirable.

Opponents and Proponents. Last, I turned to the faculty. I made a special effort to talk with the opponents, proponents, and educational policy committee members. Like the students, they seemed satisfied, but faculty were vocal about the shortcomings of written evaluations. In large classes, it was impossible to say anything about most students. In skill courses that use short-answer tests, such as introductory math and foreign language courses, one learns little about those enrolled, even if classes are small. Faculty talked about developing code words—*excellent* for A, *average* for C, and so forth. They complained that evaluations required much more work and told horror stories about students manipulating the system.

Opponents were a special case. They disliked the new grading system, and a number were still angry that it had been adopted against their objections. The result was that several graduate departments decided not to admit students from the undergraduate college who had taken more than a certain portion of their courses pass-fail. For these students, the new grading system had become a liability. It remained to be seen whether other schools or employers would discriminate against them, too.

This completed my short-term research. Three conclusions seemed inescapable. First, the new grading system had some serious shortcomings. It was far less successful than the college thought. There were problems of poor administration, abuse, misuse, and high cost. Moreover, the grading system was having a distinctly negative influence on other activities at the school, such as the undergraduate curriculum and graduate admissions.

Second, the qualitative research strategy that I used seemed to be a very good way to uncover academic problems. I was able to learn about the history and context for the new grading system, the way in which people had actually used it, and the results of their efforts. The research design that I chose permitted both a broad overview and an in-depth look at specific aspects of the grading system. It enabled me to obtain a rich mixture of subjective and objective data. Finally, it allowed me to proceed in an exploratory fashion—to know little about the subject initially and to change the research design over time as I learned more. In a period of two days, I was able to discover problems in pass-fail grading that were confirmed time and time again on campuses across the country.

Third, I concluded that institutions trying to decide whether to adopt or change a pass-fail grading system required the sort of information that I had collected to make rational decisions. The college that I visited needed what I had learned in order to upgrade its grading system. If it did not upgrade that system, the problems were quite likely to worsen. Schools that were considering a pass-fail grading system needed the information that I had collected if their deliberations were to make any sense. Too often, academic policy making at American colleges is based on anecdotes or guesses about the effects of a given proposal. The most compelling arguments seem to grow out of the experience of a friend, relative, or friend of a relative at another school where the proposal—or something like it—has already been adopted. Colleges can do better and they need to do better.

Conclusion

My example of short-term qualitative research is rather dramatic and for me somewhat atypical. Most of my research has mixed qualitative and quantitative techniques. I do not recommend one method over the other. Both have their uses. But, it is a mistake to ignore one or the other entirely. The unfortunate reality, however, is that institutional research tends to pay short shrift to qualitative research. A good deal is lost as a consequence.

Qualitative research techniques are amazingly versatile. The researcher has a whole arsenal of useful techniques—document study, observation, and interviewing—for collecting the information needed for academic decision making. All kinds of documents are available for study, ranging from institutional records and personal papers to students' tests and graffiti. I have observed—obtrusively and unobtrusively—everything from classes and meetings to dormitory and library life. As for interviews, informants have, of course, included faculty, students, and administrators. However, security staff, dining hall workers, and janitors have also been enormously helpful at times. The point is this: Qualitative research offers the investigator a great deal of flexibility and a rich array of sources to draw upon.

Observation. Here is an illustration: Typically, one of the first things that I do when I arrive at a school is to examine student notices and signs posted about the campus. I was struck by the array that I discovered at one school a few years ago. The array was predominantly political, more so that at most institutions, and that orientation I later found was reflected in the course offerings of the college. When I returned more recently, the wall decor had changed considerably. The most frequent notice posted concerned rides wanted, followed closely by record and musical sales, campus social events, such as films and guest speakers, and ads for graduate school preparation courses. Not very many political signs were in evidence anywhere. In a very real sense, these changes were a harbinger of differences that I observed subsequently in student character, course offerings, and enrollment patterns.

Another advantage of this short-term type of qualitative research is that it is cheap, easy, and fast. My study of the grading system is a good example of what one can do with little money, no staff, and only a few hours.

An Early-Warning System. An additional benefit of qualitative research, probably its greatest strength, is that it does much more than provide information needed to make decisions. In point of fact, qualitative research uncovers decisions that need to be made. My research on grading showed that all kinds of problems existed. That is important, because every problem that a school identifies entails a previously unrecognized decision that needs to be made. By becoming aware of problems when they are small, colleges can avert the crisis atmosphere that seems to accompany many of their decisions. In this sense, a continuing program of qualitative research is a good early-warning system for any school. It is a sound investment in the future.

In the final analysis, it may have been that celebrated methodologist Yogi Berra who best described the value of qualitative research. He said you can see a lot just by looking. I would only add a corollary—you can hear a lot just by listening.

Arthur Levine is a senior fellow at the Carnegie Foundation for the Advancement of Teaching in Washington, D.C.

"In my view, it would be just as sensible for the two ends of a worm to quarrel."—A. N. Whitehead's conclusion (from The Organization of Thought), *applied to "the tradition of opposition between the adherents of induction and deduction."*

Applying Qualitative Methods to Management Decisions

Michael Tierney

Whitehead's conclusion was applied to the "tradition of opposition between the adherents of induction and deduction" (Whitehead, 1967, p. 116). The same conclusion could also be applied to the tradition of opposition between the proponents of qualitative and quantitative research methods. In the case of the latter pair, the core of the problem stems from varying perspectives on what type of understanding is possible in the social sciences.

Both the quantitative and qualitative research methods stem from the collapse of German historicism in the late nineteenth century (Iggers, 1968). One line of research has its origins in Max Weber's concept of the *ideal type,* a line of research that has culminated in the development of quantitative models (Hughes, 1958). In contrast, qualitative research methods have their origins in the methods required to reach understanding of unique events. Whether it was Dilthey's *creative imagination* or Croce's *sympathetic intuition,* the goal of these methods was to understand indi-

E. Kuhns, S. V. Martorana (Eds.). *New Directions for Institutional Research: Qualitative Methods for Institutional Research,* no. 34. San Francisco: Jossey-Bass, March 1982.

vidual behavior from the point of view of the individuals involved (Hughes, 1958).

Action Meaning and Act Meaning

Consequently, there are two complementary types of understanding in the social sciences. Kaplan (1964) has labeled these two types *action meaning* and *act meaning*. Action meaning deals with what a set of acts means to social scientists. Thus, the meaning of individual behavior is provided by the particular theory being tested. Act meaning attempts to determine what the action or event signifies to the actor. In this case, perspective is provided by the values, norms, and experiences brought to the situation by the participant.

For the purposes of this chapter, attention will be confined to research methods that are particularly appropriate to discovery of the act meaning associated with the management decisions of colleges and universities. One caveat is in order. When this topic was assigned to the writer, the applicability of qualitative research methods to finance as well as to management decisions was requested. In the strict sense, finance decisions are a subset of management decisions. More specifically, finance decisions involve management decisions that determine who will share in paying for the activities and programs of colleges and universities. Thus, while subsuming finance decisions under management decisions, this chapter will focus upon the budget process of a college or university.

Qualitative Approaches to Budget Decisions

The budget decisions of such institutions have a number of salient features that make them particularly appropriate for illustrating the use of qualitative research methods. First, important budget decisions are made each and every year. From a research point of view, the annual budget cycle suggests a research design in which a number of factors, such as the principal actors, are held constant over a period of time. Employing this type of design also allows the investigator to identify decisions that reflect a real change in the institution's position. Second, and more importantly, budget decisions are both easily quantifiable and expressions of intangible institutional values and aspirations.

Figure 1 presents a simplified flowchart of trade-offs in the budget process of an hypothetical institution. This flowchart is different from the usual budget timetable guidelines developed by most colleges. The difference resides in its identifying the various decisions that have to be made in the budget process of any college, not the times when certain actions have to be taken. One important area for qualitative research is the sequence in which these decisions are made by various types of colleges. In the present example, tuition-related alternatives are tried first, followed next by attempts to retard growth in academic staff compensation. It is likely that the sequence of trade-off decisions as well as the types of trade-offs that are considered vary systematically with certain institutional characteristics.

It should be noted in passing that budget decisions generally have been studied from a variety of theoretical perspectives. Perhaps the most well known perspective is that provided by the political model (Baldridge, 1971). Pfeffer and Saloncik (1974) have applied this conceptual framework to departments that received (or lost) more resources than could be predicted by the use of such standard resource allocation rules as student credit hours and student-faculty ratios. In contrast, Cohen and March (1974) have suggested a "garbage can" model of the budget process. In this model, the various decisions in the budget cycle are loosely coupled. Consequently, budget decisions are much more likely to be made by "oversight" or even to be avoided altogether rather than by confronting value-laden issues in an ambiguous environment.

But, it is precisely these value-laden decisions that must be understood. Qualitative research methods are most appropriate for this purpose. The complex set of trade-offs illustrated in Figure 1 involves nothing more than the ranking of different values held by various participants in the budget process. Two such trade-offs will now be considered in more detail: tuition revenues and academic staff compensation.

Tuition Revenues. There are essentially two ways of increasing an institution's tuition revenues: Increase the level of tuition itself while holding enrollment constant, or increase enrollment while holding tuition constant. The question of how these two factors are combined is a question of values.

Imagine the dean of the faculty arguing the pros and cons of holding enrollment constant while increasing tuition more rapidly

84

Figure 1. Institutional Trade-Offs

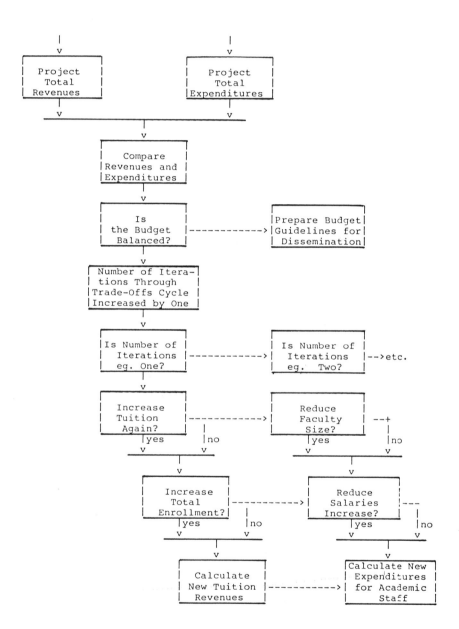

than originally anticipated. The dean lists three arguments in favor of this particular set of trade-offs:

- "By not becoming larger, we avoid the deleterious impact of crowding on the quality of life on campus."
- "Opportunities for formal and informal interactions among faculty and students would be maintained."
- "The net incremental revenues available to the institution would be increased substantially."

Against these generally positive outcomes would be the little-understood impact of tuition increases on the probability that prospective applicants would apply to, much less matriculate at, the college. Thus, the dean's arguments against such a set of trade-offs might include the following:

- "The diversity of entering classes would be reduced, thereby limiting the advantages of a pluralistic campus community."
- "The college would have to admit more students with lower academic achievement in order to offset the small decline in the number of matriculants caused by the tuition increase."
- "The institution's overall position relative to its competitors would be diminished."

By deciding on this particular combination, the dean of the faculty reveals preferences for continuing student-faculty interactions on the same level over the possible deleterious effects of a tuition increase on a diverse student body.

Academic Staff Compensation. As indicated in Figure 1, reductions in academic staff compensation would be required if the college budget still did not balance after a second round of tuition increases. Again, imagine the dean of the faculty's arguing for a reduction in the number of faculty positions through "orderly" attrition while leaving anticipated salary increases unaltered. The dean lists three arguments in favor of these decisions:

- "Maintaining the proposed salary increases significantly enhances our ability to attract and retain the quality of faculty that is the cornerstone of our academic program."
- "Faculty morale, particularly among junior faculty, is maintained."
- "Significant cost savings can be realized, particularly over the long run."

Against these benefits are the patent negative outcomes for the institution's academic program, especially in specific teaching situations. Thus, two possible arguments against this set of trade-offs are these:

- "Reductions in the size of the academic staff, when coupled with a constant level of enrollment, marks a deterioration in student-teacher relationships."
- "Teaching and advising workloads in some departments may become so high as to affect adversely the morale of faculty and the overall quality of programs in those departments."

In deciding on this particular combination, the dean's preference for attracting and retaining a faculty of desired quality outweighs concerns for the potential harm that reductions in the size of faculty could have on student-teacher interactions.

It would be easy to expand the examples concerning these types of decisions. For instance, how would the dean of the faculty at this hypothetical institution weigh the costs and benefits of a tuition increase against a reduction in the proposed faculty salary increase? Would the dean pay the faculty to teach, or would the dean pay students to enroll, either by direct financial assistance or by less than inflationary increases in tuition? Whatever the example, administrators annually make such trade-offs when balancing institutional budgets.

Several possible institutional benefits emerge from the study of what these decisions mean to participants in the decision-making process. Studying the relative value that different participants attach to such factors as fiscal solvency, academic program quality, and faculty morale can help to identify possible areas of conflict among senior administrators. Such identification can lead to a variety of organizational development techniques to reduce this conflict. In the case of consensus among decision makers, one comes to understand some of the reasons for the inertia in institutional budgets. Awareness of this consensus should inform senior administrators of the direction in which the institution is headed and lead them to ask whether they are willing to live with the consequences.

Conclusion

Thus, it is as important to study what the decisions mean to a group of decision makers as it is to determine what trade-offs are finally made. Colleges and universities are, after all, collections of people who hold diverse and sometimes conflicting sets of values. As colleges move into the 1980s, questions of what an institution is becoming will be as important as the institution's ability to remain fiscally solvent. From the perspective of budget-balancing trade-offs, the anticipated demographically induced enrollment decline is as much a problem of institutional aspirations about the scale and scope of its academic programs as it is a recruitment and admissions issue. Qualitative research methods, when applied with care and rigor, can play an important role in charting an institution's course through these difficult decisions.

References

Baldridge, J. V. *Power and Conflict in the University*. New York: Wiley, 1971.

Cohen, M., and March, J. G. *Leadership and Ambiguity*. New York: McGraw-Hill, 1974.

Hughes, H. S. *Consciousness and Society*. New York: Vintage Books, 1958.

Iggers, G. G. *The German Conception of History*. Middletown, Conn.: Wesleyan University Press, 1968.

Kaplan, A. *The Conduct of Inquiry*. New York: Chandler, 1964.

Pfeffer, J., and Saloncik, G. R. "Organizational Decision Making as a Political Process: In Case of the University Budget." *Administrative Science Quarterly*, 1974, *19*, 135–151.

Whitehead, A. N. *The Aims of Education and Other Essays*. New York: Free Press, 1967.

Michael Tierney is an associate professor and assistant director of the Higher Education Finance Research Institute at the University of Pennsylvania.

*Faculty members need the perspectives
and knowledge that derive from educational
research, and researchers need the connections
with faculty members if their findings are
to affect practice.*

Qualitative Research Methods and Educational Practice

Jerry Gaff

Despite a dramatic expansion of research on education during recent decades, we seem not to be much wiser than we were, nor has the abundance of educational research led, as many expected, to improvements in educational practice. Important gains in understanding have been made, to be sure, and they should be celebrated. Much has been learned about college faculties and other groups within higher education, as well as about the organization and functioning of colleges and universities. This research has resulted in a body of factual information that was previously not available.

However, there are serious limitations to this research. First, the research is typically pointed more toward an empirical description of the educational system than toward an idealized vision of the system as it could be. Second, the research seldom deals with basic ideas or concepts, in part because such concepts tend to be large with meaning, ambiguous, and difficult to pin down to operational definitions. Third, much of the research is undertaken for its own sake, divorced from considerations for action. Characteris-

E. Kuhns, S. V. Martorana (Eds.). *New Directions for Institutional Research: Qualitative Methods for Institutional Research*, no. 34. San Francisco: Jossey-Bass, March 1982.

tically, it is conducted by professional researchers who address academic concerns of the research community and disseminate the results to fellow researchers; this leaves practitioners more or less out of the picture. Fourth, this research seldom leads to actual improvements. Because piecemeal empirical studies by themsleves do not point conclusively to any one route to improvement, researchers understandably are reluctant to endorse any specific change. So severe are these criticisms that innovators with whom I have worked have developed a rule of thumb: Whenever educational researchers get involved in a reform movement, the action is over. Research follows rather than stimulates innovations. It is not accidental that most of the research in question is quantitative.

Most of the limitations just named can be overcome with an infusion of qualitative research. Especially needed is qualitative research that embraces a vision of a better educational world, focuses on basic concepts, forges explicit links to practice, and synthesizes studies that collectively can point to specific improvements.

Faculty members are the central actors in the education of students and the most important resource for strengthening an educational program. Their ideas, values, and behaviors are pivotal in an understanding of education and in making changes. Faculty usually derive their ideas about educational practice from folklore conveyed by their own teachers, professional colleagues, and the cultures of their academic disciplines. Few have developed their ideas by systematic study of the results of educational research. The consequence of this state of affairs is that naive, simplistic, and sometimes downright erroneous ideas about teaching and learning abound. A casual visit to virtually any faculty lounge can provide ample documentation for this statement. Such circumstances make faculty members ripe for enlightenment by educational research, particularly the kind that encourages them to conceptualize their own views, subject these views to critical analysis and test them in practice, and consider alternatives that may be able to help them achieve their own purposes. In short, faculty members need the perspectives and knowledge that derive from educational research, and researchers need the connections with faculty members if their findings are to affect practice. Each group needs the other. They can be joined together by rigorous study of educational ideas that are examined through research, including qualitative aspects.

These abstractions can be illustrated by some of my own research in three different areas—cluster colleges, faculty development, and general education. Each of these foci of research represents different approaches to the improvement of undergraduate education. Following the discussion of my own writing, I will identify several principles of qualitative research that can be derived from these studies.

Cluster Colleges

Cluster colleges were ideal innovations for the growth-oriented 1960s. As the baby boom of the post–World War II years produced college-age youth, educational policies were formulated to accommodate the increased numbers. The most common and easiest response was to do business as usual and merely expand existing institutions. Another response was to create new institutions. For a time, more than one college a week was founded, virtually all of which seemed to come from the same mold. However, a few thinkers worried that important values were being sacrificed in the headlong rush to expand, and they conceived an alternative scheme, by which a college could grow larger while growing smaller. It was to grow by creating a cluster of small semiautonomous colleges in an American adaptation of the Oxford-Cambridge organizational pattern, an old idea but new to the times and the context.

This form of organization has several advantages over the conventionally structured institution of higher learning. First, because the cluster college is by definition small, it can create a closer community, offer more personalized instruction, and foster warmer student-faculty relations than the large centralized institution. Second, a university composed of several separate colleges, each with a different undergraduate program, provides the structural diversity needed to cope with the wide range of individual differences of an ever-increasing number of students. Third, the cluster college provides a mechanism by which a university can experiment on a limited basis with new philosophies and approaches to education. Fourth, the spirit of innovation generated in the cluster college can spread and provoke reforms in other portions of the university. Finally, because the cluster college can tap the central facilities and services of the university, it has access to rich intellectual and cultural resources at comparatively low cost.

I was able to pull together many isolated experiments, explain the rationale behind them, describe variations in structures at different institutions, and assemble some of the early evidence— both quantitative and qualitative—to validate the cluster concept (Gaff, 1970).

Faculty Development

The 1970s brought new challenges. Growth was slowing, and the dread villains of retrenchment, steady state, and financial exigency were sighted. How, we asked, are we to keep our faculties alive and our institutions vital in the coming years? The answer of many was faculty development (Berquist and Phillips, 1975; Lindquist, 1978; Gaff, Festa and Gaff, 1978; Gaff, 1978). However, this was not the common sort of faculty development that involved research support, travel to professional meetings, and general updating and upgrading of specialized knowledge. More comprehensive changes were needed, changes that embraced larger portions of the individual personality, that renewed the entire institution, and that invigorated the instructional program. New programs of faculty development or teaching improvement based on new assumptions were invented. These programs assumed that faculty are committed to teaching and want to excel in it; that institutions can do more to encourage excellent teaching and the full development of individual faculty members; that there are many different ways to enhance professional performance, none of which works for all people or all schools; that the carrot, not the stick, is the most promising way to bring about improvements; and that every institution has a rich pool of talented individuals that can be used to promote the development of all. None of these assumptions is new, but, as with the cluster college concept, the new concept of faculty development pointed to departures from prevailing practice that promised to deal with the new configuration of problems. Again, I was able to synthesize much of the pioneering activity on a variety of college campuses, articulate alternative concepts that were being used to promote renewal (faculty, instructional, and organizational development), describe different institutional arrangements to support these efforts, and summarize the early evidence that validated the concept (Gaff, 1975).

Curriculum Reform

On the edge of the 1980s, yet another set of problems appeared: Students were discovered to be poorly educated, and the curriculum seemed to be at fault, especially the general education portion of the curriculum (Carnegie Foundation for the Advancement of Teaching, 1977; Boyer and Levine, 1981; Gaff, 1982). The system of loose distribution requirements found on most campuses was declared a disaster area, and several thinkers called for a return to a common core. Large numbers of institutions have discovered that they had problems, and hundreds today are conducting reviews or revising their programs. As with other reforms, different institutions adopt different structures. Some attend to skills, whether basic skills, such as reading, writing, and arithmetic, or advanced skills, such as analytic, synthetic, or critical thinking. Other institutions are requiring more study of liberal arts subjects and imposing more structure in their distribution scheme. Still others stress integration of knowledge, critical analysis of values and value implications of knowledge, global studies including non-Western areas, and the like. For the last three years, I have directed the Project on General Education Models, which worked with twelve different institutions as they tried to strengthen the core of their undergraduate curriculum. New concepts of general education involving more than breadth, more than a distribution scheme were developed and shared; action research was conducted to make a case for change; resource materials, including a distillation of the professional literature and an annotated bibliography on some of the most useful items, were prepared; alternative curricular configurations were devised and adopted; and an assessment of the lessons learned from the early experiences on a number of campuses was conducted.

Eight Principles

These three examples are not offered as models of effective qualitative research. In fact, each combines qualitative with quantitative approaches. However, from these examples, eight general principles for enhancing research by including qualitative aspects may be derived.

First, consider the larger context. In each of the three examples presented here, the national context changed dramatically—from growth, to retrenchment, to a concern for quality. Those who were able to anticipate future problems and fashion productive ways of addressing them helped to shape institutional responses. It is essential to understand the institutional context as well, because colleges and universities adapted cluster colleges, faculty development programs, and general education curricula to fit their own circumstances. Understanding any one of these concepts in a single institutional setting is useful, but studying their variations in different institutions gives depth and richness to each of the concepts.

Second, focus on key concepts. The cluster college, faculty development, and general education are ideas that have multiple meanings. Although each concept embraces a large number of values, ideas, and practices, some of which are conflicting, all are sufficiently specific to focus study and experimentation on a limited area. Further, each idea combines the qualities of timelessness with timeliness; this lends all three ideas enduring as well as contemporary significance. Indeed, their very ambiguity allows them to function as an umbrella under which many like-minded individuals can gather to reinforce one another, share ideas and experiences, and generate a sense of participation in a movement that is larger than any one.

Third, present a vision of what education could reasonably be. The concept of a university with a differentiated structure that permits several alternative colleges to coexist on the same campus is an appealing one. It has persisted since 1249 and the founding of Oxford University. The ideal of effective teachers who work to perfect their craft and whose continual development is supported by their institutions is also attractive and will remain so even after the specific circumstances that gave rise to the recent pressure for faculty development dissipate. Similarly, the ideal of providing a broad general education to students, whatever their field of specialization or career preference may be, is enduring. Although these three ideals can be defined in many different ways, all three embrace educational values shared by many.

Fourth, compare that vision with current practice, and make a case for change. In each of the examples cited here, current practice falls short of the ideal. With regard to general education, evidence, both qualitative and quantitative, abounds that many students are poorly skilled, narrowly trained, and not well equipped to cope with the demands of the future. A curriculum committee at one of the twelve institutions which were in our project decided to assess the effectiveness of the current curriculum and surveyed students, faculty, alumni, and course-taking patterns. While the evidence was largely quantitative, committee members interpreted it not in and of itself but in order to test their normative concept of a generally educated student. The group used the several studies to make a case for change. The evidence said, "We can do better."

Fifth, look for exemplary programs to highlight. Quantitative researchers almost automatically assume that a good study requires a random sample. If they are studying the curriculum in community colleges, for example, they think that it is important to study a representative sample that allows them to generalize their findings to all community colleges. However, if the purpose is to highlight effective alternatives, it can be more useful to study a few exemplary programs. In the case of a survey that I am conducting now, we are trying to learn about the kinds of changes that are emerging from the recent wave of reform in general education. Rather than surveying a sample of all institutions, which would probably reveal relatively little change and most of that not very imaginative, we are surveying a purposive sample of schools that are known to be making revisions. This will give us a sense of what schools that are actively working in this area have come up with, and it will include many of the most interesting examples. If things go as planned, the results should stretch the imagination of some readers and stimulate research-inspired improvements.

Sixth, create a network of practitioners to advance their programmatic purposes while contributing to the advance of knowledge. So often, a researcher studies individuals who are not involved in defining the issues and who therefore have little ownership of the results. But, if the task is both to study change and to facilitate change, researchers need to bring practitioners into the study when deciding what questions to ask. The results of the research will then have a claim on the attention of persons in the program. It will either reinforce their practices or help them to make mid-course corrections that improve their efforts. In either event, studying and doing can be intimately connected. Each can help to advance the purposes of researchers and practitioners.

Seventh, see that the results are utilized. Frequently, re-searchers conduct a study, write up the results, and that is the end of it. They are reticent to share their results with others or to impose their ideas on others. But, the researcher who wants to make a difference, one who wants to realize the educational values that infuse his studies, has a more active role to play. The researcher's evidence, its interpretation, and its use in decision making can play a crucial role in actualizing the educational vision that informs the researcher's study. Researchers have an obligation not only to conduct their studies professionally but to make sure that their data are interpreted fairly and utilized prop-erly. This can mean taking the initiative to provide feedback to those who provided information as well as to others with a vested interest in the results and their implications. In some cases, this can mean taking an advocacy position, if that is what the data demon-strate. Although this prospect is feared by many researchers as compromising their objectivity, there is little harm in defending such values as faculty renewal or a generally educated student body.

Eighth, combine qualitative and quantitative methods. Neither one has a claim to infallibility or to universal utility. Both have a role to play. In the three examples that constitute the basis for this chapter, both kinds of evidence have been utilized to under-stand the larger context, frame a vision of better education, make a case for improvement, and enlighten practitioners about the con-sequences of their efforts. In most instances, what is needed today is to redress the balance by increasing the role of qualitative ideas and evidence. However, if the pendulum swings too far in the other direction, we could wind up with an abundance of ideas and obser-vations that are not supported by numbers and other hard data. That would be equally unfortunate.

Conclusion

The argument of this chapter is that attention paid to qual-itative aspects can make research in higher education more effec-tive. Indeed, we could even refer to such research as *scholarship,* a proud if quaint word in this field. Such scholarship, following some of the principles identified above, could once again embrace ideals, purposes, and values in a legitimate fashion; it could con-nect key ideas with actions; and it could help to point the way to improvements in practice. These changes could allow scholarship and scholars to regain the lead in shaping the character of higher education.

References

Bergquist, W. H., and Phillips, S. R. "Components of an Effective Faculty Development Program." *Journal of Higher Education,* 1975, 177–211.
Boyer, E. L., and Levine, A. *A Quest for Common Learning.* Washington, D.C.: Carnegie Foundation for the Advancement of Teaching, 1981.
Carnegie Foundation for the Advancement of Teaching. *Missions of the College Curriculum: A Contemporary Review with Suggestions.* San Francisco: Jossey-Bass, 1977.
Gaff, J. *The Cluster College.* San Francisco: Jossey-Bass, 1970.
Gaff, J. *Toward Faculty Renewal: Advances in Faculty, Instructional, and Organizational Development.* San Francisco: Jossey-Bass, 1975.
Gaff, J. (Ed.). *New Directions for Higher Education: Institutional Renewal Through the Improvement of Teaching,* no. 24. San Francisco: Jossey-Bass, 1978.
Gaff, J., Festa, C., and Gaff, S. *Professional Development: A Guide to Resources.* New Rochelle, N.Y.: Change Magazine Press, 1978.
Gaff, J., Festa, C., and Gaff, S. *Reconstructing General Education.* San Francisco: Jossey-Bass, in press.
Lindquist, J. (Ed.). *Designing Teaching Improvement Programs.* Washington, D.C.: Council of Independent Colleges, 1978.

Jerry Gaff is working on curriculum projects for the Association of American Colleges. He has directed national projects on the cluster college, faculty development, and curriculum reform. Currently, he is writing a book on the most promising new approaches to improving the quality of general education.

Determining what is valid and what is
questionable when assessing quality is the
$64,000 question.

Measuring Indicators
of Quality

George W. Bonham

Consistent with the design of this volume, the authors of the preceding chapters have concentrated on the role of institutional research in improving institutional decision making and on how effective use of qualitative methods of academic inquiry can further this process. The purpose of this concluding chapter is to carry the discussion beyond issues contingent to the choice of appropriate methodology. Instead, it seeks to focus the reader's attention on determination of significant issues on which policy decisions now seem to be unclear or in need of redirection. Only when this critical determination is appreciated by both the leaders who make the decisions and the institutional researchers who strive to build the knowledge base can expectations to improve the enterprise be realistically fulfilled.

Whatever the methodology chosen to measure quality indicators in the educational process, academic managers and institutional researchers alike should not permit themselves the luxury of assuming that such constructs and measurement instruments function in a vacuum. Educational policymakers, despite some protestations to the contrary, do not work in a science-neutral

E. Kuhns, S. V. Martorana (Eds.). *New Directions for Institutional Research: Qualitative Methods for Institutional Research*, no. 34. San Francisco: Jossey-Bass, March 1982.

environment. It will even be argued by some that the very choice of a particular methodology may be value laden, thus affecting the research outcome.

Defining appropriate quality methodologies would be relatively simple, were traditional elements such as quality teaching and a stimulating curriculum the only criteria for judging learning outcomes. As Diane Ravitch of Columbia University's Teachers College put it recently, "we expect the schools to teach children command of the fundamental skills that are needed to continue learning—in particular, the ability to read, write, compute, speak, and listen. Once they have command of these skills, they should progress through a curriculum designed to enlarge their powers. . . . The curriculum should be designed so that every student has the fullest opportunity to develop his powers, intelligence, interests, talent, and understanding" (Ravitch, 1981, pp. 329–340).

The above seem to be the public expectations of the educational enterprise. But it is arguable also that a certain randomness of unmeasurable influences make cause and effect judgments within the ecosphere of formal educational settings almost impossible. Quality instruction and a learner-oriented curriculum are functions and consequences of institutional determination. The myriad external influences on the learner are not statistically measurable.

Since one of the most desirable outcomes of effective learning environments must be the learner's own self-sufficiency, the influences and effects of teaching and curriculum may, in time, be more an adjunct rather than the principal effect of the learning efficiency of the student. As Benjamin Bloom puts it, "if maximum quality of instruction is provided in the early learning tasks in a series and most of the learners attain mastery of these learning tasks, something less than maximal quality of instruction appears to be needed in the later learning tasks in the series to ensure mastery of these later tasks. Thus, the generalization appears to be that students can acquire learning procedures which will enable them to learn well under less than ideal qualities of instruction (Bloom, 1976, p. 135).

It is clear that educational researchers should pursue the eminently worthwhile objectives of measuring quality indicators in the educational process but with considerable humility. This is due to the convergence of the relativistic nature of multiple learning influences and the fact that social and cognitive science research is not conducted in some hermetically sealed vacuum. Organizational policy decisions should, of course, rely in substantial measure on information that can be gathered using quantitative or qualitative procedures. But the added value functions that the college experience can impart to students are not the only ones reflected in such measurements; also reflected are the less easily defined functions of a student's nonintellectual development. One must appreciate the virtue of hunches as well as the results of our assessment techniques.

We now turn to the broader reaches of the more public issues involved in these questions. By what quality measurements are we to consider institutional and public action? After all, what is one man's foible may well be another man's birthright. What seem to be quality issues in the public mind may not be quality issues for professional educators. For example what is popularly meant by back to basics is not necessarily what is thought to be important by sophisticated educators, and the educational efficiency that state legislators may demand of their public institutions is often not valued by those in our schools and colleges.

The difficulty of considering policy questions on quality issues is further compounded by traditional academic assumptions, which may or may not be valid. At the risk of excommunication, I venture a short list of those sacred cows. Academic institutions measure themselves qualitatively by some of the following indices: student-faculty ratios, library acquisitions and collections, number of faculty Ph.D.s, size and variety of college course offerings, number of resident students, number of baccalaureates continuing on to graduate schools, per-student instructional expenditures, size of endowment, and number of faculty research publications. In the perfect world, all these indices, if maximized to their ultimate, would produce an extraordinary institution, which would produce exceptionally well-educated students. Or would they? They would not. None of these traditional measures of quality guarantees a quality education.

Perhaps this is not the occasion to criticize some of the academy's sacred cows. Suffice it to say that if one is to base institutional decisions on qualitative data, we must first agree on what data are valid and what data are questionable. Surely, great teachers are not necessarily those who have earned a doctoral degree. Measuring the value of libraries by the number of volumes has no relationship to the quality of their holdings. The overall quality of faculty cannot be measured merely by tallying their publications or the campus committees on which they serve. Per-student investments frequently bear little relationship to educational output. As Howard Bowen (1980) pointed out, the range of differences in cost per student is astonishing, even among institutions with similar educative missions.

Why, then, when the task seems so difficult, have we seen this surge of interest within the past decade in measuring quality, or the lack thereof, and acting on these determinations? The initiatives, it must be said, come as much from external sources as from anywhere else. Money surely lies at the heart of this issue as does the general lowering of standards brought about by the wider inclusion of new learners from intellectually less-favored backgrounds. While I think that we ought not to take declining SAT scores as the sole and most reliable cause of our discontent, we would be living in a fool's paradise if we believed that mass and class education can in time coincide. Sooner or later, the inevitable truth is revealed that not every college in the nation holds its good share of academic talent. Demographics do not lie, and somebody has to take the shale. But, for an institution to admit that it is scraping the bottom of the barrel can be psychologically heartbreaking and also damaging to students. So, we talk about quality, but we act on the harsh exigencies of academic survival. What is far more unsettling in both the moral and the intellectual sense is that we may ignore the possibility that the so-called marginal colleges, which deal with so-called marginal students, may do more educationally for individual students than many Ivy League schools. The best potential for net educational improvement lies toward the bottom of the bell curve, not at its top. One could well take a value-added approach to quality issues in education.

We must thus distinguish between acknowledgement of the facts of declining quality in American education and our effective ability to quantify quality with sufficient reliability. The first is far easier than the second. My own fear is that we may so obscure the issue of enhancing educational quality by our attempts to quantify it through obscurantist social science stratagems that we find ourselves even further behind than we already are. Unfortunately for the measurers, the great moments of human discoveries, insights, and creativity are rarely embodied in institutional research. I have seen too many splendid learning environments that, in their almost accidental uniqueness, relied heavily on one great college president or one great teacher. By and large, quantitative analysis passes over such human quality-generators. Any quantitative analysis of Black Mountain College would have destined it to the rubbish heap long before its natural time for extinction. We only have a poor memory of how great human works and institutions can be, no matter how unassuming they are in their measurable structure.

What, then, of complaints that the general level of education is declining to a point where remedial action is essential? Some of these indictments seem fully justified. Texas Commissioner Kenneth H. Ashworth (1979) puts the matter simply: "While not all changes in our colleges have been for the worse, we are permitting predictable courses of events to proceed unchecked to the detriment of quality in higher education. Continued deterioration of quality, in turn, will result in a loss of public support, upon which higher education is acutely dependent. When the public is fickle and higher education enters the courtship without principle, our colleges and universities are going to be used and taken advantage of and will end up with the reputation that they do not deserve respect" (Ashworth, 1979, pp. 19–20).

Thoughtful state education leaders like Commissioner Ashworth have stood in the forefront of those who have expressed concerns about decline in educational quality. As quintessential egalitarians, they stand in curious partnership with elitist scholars who have long thought that education has fallen to the philistines. In a recent study of ten California colleges for the California Postsecondary Education Commission, Bowen and Glenny (1980) provide a timely warning: "To do more than simply survive, colleges and universities must maintain program quality through policies and processes that impose order on uncertainty to the extent possible. It would be foolish to predict that the most effective procedures will improve the quality of existing programs, but honest assessment of program quality, priorities, and staffing can afford at least a small measure of assurance that student needs will be met as they arise" (Bowen and Glenny, 1980, pp. 61–62).

The disturbing relationships between declining resources and the necessary maintenance of educational quality are examined in a recent Southern Regional Education Board (1981) monograph, *The Need for Quality:* "With enrollment declines on the horizon, colleges may be tempted to abandon or reject higher standards for admission and retention of students. How much attention may colleges be expected to pay to excellence when they

are fighting for survival with budgets based on student counts? . . .
These factors underscore the urgency to make educational improvements, which are unlikely to take place without wide-scale cooperation among all levels of education. Continued duplication of
efforts, ineffective programs that do not meet their objectives, rigid
institutional arrangements that do not fit today's reality, in short,
the luxury of 'business as usual,' cannot continue to prevail"
(pp. 1–2).

If money were not in short supply, it is doubtful that the
issue of quality would now be raised as insistently as it is. It
once seemed possible to deal with quality questions by throwing
money after the problem or simply by papering the problem over
with surface solutions. My own interests in these quality issues
came to the fore while I was editor-in-chief of *Change* magazine. I
decided to sponsor a fresh analysis of financial analyses of institutional health. The results were released and published in 1976
(Lupton, Augenblick, and Heyison, 1976). The study was met with
a general disbelief that an effort to measure the financial health of
institutions could seriously be attempted. Nonetheless, this study
helped to renew research efforts on many fronts to measure the
fiscal health of higher education. My own concern about this study
was not for its methodology or its outcomes. Instead, it involved a
basic question that I should have asked and did not ask: Even if the
books are balanced, what has been silently sacrificed in academic
quality? It was the $64,000 question and far more difficult to
quantify.

In one pilot attempt to answer some of these quality questions, we encouraged the Higher Educational Research Institute to
develop reputational ratings of academic institutions without distinguished graduate programs (Solmon and Astin, 1981a, 1981b).
Whether one agrees that reputational ranking studies are valid or
not, the selected indices of quality that emerged are interesting in
themselves: overall quality of undergraduate education, preparation for graduate school, preparation for employment, faculty
commitment to undergraduate teaching, scholarly accomplish-
ments of faculty, and innovativeness of the curriculum. Departments of undergraduate colleges were ranked in seven fields. The
authors describe one of their major findings this way: "While we
have been able to show how these reputational ratings are related
to a variety of other institutional characteristics, we have not
explored the more fundamental question of how 'quality,' as

reflected in such expert judgments, is related to the educational development of the student. Do students in highly rated undergraduate institutions develop differently from students in institutions with mediocre or low ratings? In other words, while we have been able to operationalize the 'quality folklore' in the form of reputational ratings, we have not as yet tested the validity of that folklore, that is, that attending a highly regarded institution is supposed to confer special educational benefits on the student. Clearly, such 'value-added' studies would aid greatly in our efforts to understand and strengthen institutional quality" (Solomon and Astin, 1981b, p. 19).

Reputational surveys, of course, have their assorted shortcomings. But, still assuming the presence of an entrepreneurial and competitive spirit in the academic vineyards, it is just possible that such peer measurement can stir faculties and administrations into action. Comparing oneself against the best, or indeed against national or regional norms, can have good side effects if one happens to be below the line and wants to move up. The important issue here is to shape and carve out strong institutional beliefs in what constitute the quality issues for a particular place at a particular time. And that takes, above all, holding on to some pivotal perspectives.

From the perspective of our civic and intellectual ideal, relatively few students can be said to be the beneficiaries of the best that education has to offer. In the civic sense, relatively few students are sufficiently exposed to such essential areas as moral development, cognitive and analytic literacy, appropriate understanding of modern science, even of basic economics and human understanding. In fact, quality issues of such kinds already press so hard on the curricular structure of the most motivated colleges that one can only wonder what can replace what and at what attendant costs and losses.

In short, quality questions can be raised to almost infinite levels. I don't know of any academic institution, no matter how rich or imaginative, that can successfully fill all the qualitative gaps and lapses that the human experience needs to attend to.

Such are some of the macroquality questions. Measured largely by instinct and the general social happiness or malaise, they are difficult tests of quality by the very reason of their all-embracing character. But, even at the micro level, the measurement of quality has much to do with peer beliefs and general anthropo-

logical aspects of campus life. Among the most persistent of the
questions that have been answered at the micro level is the issue of
teacher quality. Several aspects of academic practice make such
quality determinations hazardous at best. Both the primacy and
privacy of the teacher in his and her classroom is one such aspect.
Pedagogic skills divorced from competence in one's field is
another. Dubious students' evaluations of teachers is surely a third,
while the drumming up of enrollments may have more to do with
teacher popularity than it does with intellectual effectiveness.

"Among the most pervasive obstacles to the development of
a quality system of teaching," writes Hans O. Mauksch (1980), a
former executive head of the American Sociological Association,
"is the belief that the teacher's performance is primarily a reflection of the teacher's talent and native gifts. Held as a pervasive belief, the notion that teachers are born rather than educated
is central to an observation of teacher careers and teacher
employment."

Mauksch's sensitive analysis of quality issues in teaching is
worth repeating:

> Let us compare the teacher and the violinist. For the
> latter, society has accepted the coexistence of learned com-
> petence and individually achieved excellence. The social
> and institutional environment of the violinist requires,
> encourages, and rewards efforts to learn, to practice, to work
> hard, and to achieve competence as a direct outcome of dili-
> gence. We also recognize that, among those who achieve
> competence, there is a range of endowment and talent and
> that, beyond the level of competence, a selected few will
> reach a level of excellence which is an individual and
> unique achievement. Achieving competence is based on
> social arrangements and a socially expected and rewarded
> pathway of learning. The postsecondary higher education
> field lacks beliefs, arrangements, and encouragement to
> achieve teaching competence through deliberate learning
> efforts. On the contrary, such efforts are devalued, if not
> disparaged. Unlike the violinist, who achieves competence
> through learning and work, the teacher is thought to be-
> come competent as a semianointed by-product of the doc-
> toral degree. Without rewards for those who work at the
> teaching process, the academic community expects the

virtuoso, the unique talent, to arise and shine in the classroom.

Performing, be it as violinist or teacher, combines competence in the performing process with expertise in the substantive area, be it music or one of the academic arts and sciences. Expertise in theories of music and knowledge of every violin sonata does not make for a competent performance with the bow. Without adequate training with the instrument, no one would expect the expert to be a performer. Yet, this is precisely what we do in the academic community. Presumed knowledge of a subject matter is a license to teach without acknowledging that the teacher's instrument, the use of himself or herself, requires skills and practice. The belief systems surrounding the nature of teaching and the arrangements by which teachers are selected and employed practically prevent the development and maintenance of a cadre of competent teachers. It has not blocked the emergence of those few masters of the classroom who, overcoming absence of training and support systems, perform as individual virtuosos. The crucial consequences of these beliefs lie in the absence of effective social arrangements to require, encourage, and reward the acquisition of teaching competence for the bulk of those who teach. These beliefs have supported norms which make it undesirable, if not embarrassing, to admit that learning about teaching ought to be a good thing (Mauksch, 1980, pp. 1-3).

The difficulty of measuring quality aspects of teaching is just one of the more confounding issues before education in a generally confounding age. For, if one is hard put to measure the quality of one's essential product, how is one to compete effectively in a highly competitive marketplace? The only useful advice under these circumstances is extreme caution. Many circumstantial things must happen if such measurements are to take on useful substance and reliability, particularly when significant strategy changes are a result of such determinations.

Hayden Smith, an economist and senior vice-president of the Council for Financial Aid to Education, puts the analytic problems of determining academic quality this way:

The term *quality* implies a sense of ordering or valuation by which one thing can be judged to be better than or worse than another thing. Institutional quality in teaching and learning bears the same implication. And, this applies both to interinstitutional comparisons and to intertemporal comparisons. The aggregation of dissimilar input factors implies a weighting process or system which depends on either a demonstrably objective standard, which does not yet exist, or a set of subjective values. It would appear, then, that the measurement of educational quality by means of an aggregation of inputs does not escape the problem of subjectivity.

The same can be said for the use of outputs. Educational outcomes or products are conceptually even more difficult to deal with than inputs. The characteristics of students graduating, their achievement scores, and their postgraduate records in terms of position, salary, or other attainments all bear the defect that they reflect not only the educational quality of the institution but also the characteristics of the students themselves at the time of matriculation. Is the superior quality often attributed to the graduates of Ivy League colleges a function of the superior quality of those institutions, or is it a function of the selectivity of those schools in their admission policies and practices? Clearly, the outcome of an educational process in terms of the absolute attributes of a graduating student are very much reflective of the absolute attributes possessed by that student at the beginning of the process (Smith, 1981, p. 3).

Having said all that, how can decision makers gather the facts about quality issues that seem to matter the most? I would first look at the broader academic circumstances, on which all else really depends. These circumstances would surely include general public attitudes toward education. There is not much that one can do about them, but decisions on quality issues will hinge in part on the prevailing public mood.

Second, one must be mindful of the qualitative erosion that is brought about by declining institutional morale, a relative drop in faculty earnings, the current student sociology of consummate career-mindedness, growing public disinterest in educational matter, and the overall question of staff competence. The fat is gone from most academic institutions, but the new lean circumstances have not necessarily brought greater institutional effectiveness. There is necessary organizational slack in any collegial system, but there is also along a broad spectrum of nonprofit institutions, a pattern of sheer incompetence in ways that mattered little in earlier times.

With but rare exceptions, the measurement of quality in educational institutions can at best result in positive but only incremental changes. If the presidency of the United States is limited both in real powers and in the general ability to move matters significantly, this is nothing compared with the general limitations on presidents of academic institutions. Quantitative leaps toward excellence are rather unlikely here, although one ought not to underestimate the possibility of generally raising the qualitative environment by both internal and external initiatives that will go largely unmeasured and that will remain unmeasurable.

So, one is largely locked in by circumstances beyond the control of academic decision makers. But, belief in the general ability of educational institutions to improve their quality components must inevitably remain a centerpiece of academic life.

References

Ashworth, H. M. *American Higher Education in Decline.* College Station: Texas A&M Press, 1979.

Bloom, B. S. *Human Characteristics and School Learning.* New York: McGraw-Hill, 1976.

Bowen, H. R. *The Costs of Higher Education: How Much Do Colleges and Universities Spend per Student and How Much Should They Spend?* San Francisco: Jossey-Bass, 1980.

Bowen, H. R., and Glenny, L. A. *Uncertainty in Public Higher Education.* Sacramento: California Postsecondary Education Commission, 1980.

Lupton, A. H., Augenblick, J., and Heyison, J. "The Financial State of Higher Education." *Change,* 1976, *8* (8), p. 21.

Mauksch, H. O. Speech made to the National Conference of American Association for Higher Education, March 6, 1980.

Ravitch, D. "Forgetting the Questions! The Problem of Educational Reform." *The American Scholar,* 1981, *50* (3), 329-40.

Smith, H. W. "Reflections on Educational Quality, with Special Reference to the United States in the 1980s." Unpublished manuscript.

Solmon, L. C., and Astin, A. W. "A New Study of Excellence in Undergraduate Education. Part One: Departments Without Distinguished Graduate Programs." *Change,* 1981a, *13* (6), p. 22.

Solmon, L. C., and Astin, A. W. "A New Study of Excellence in Undergraduate Education. Part Two: The Quality of Undergraduate Education—Are Reputational Ratings Needed to Measure Quality?" *Change,* 1981b, *13* (7), p. 19.

110

Southern Regional Education Board. *The Need for Quality.* Atlanta: Southern Regional Education Board, 1981.

George W. Bonham is executive director of the Council on Learning and editor-at-large of Change *magazine.*

*A summary of the contributions of various
disciplines to qualitative methodology and the
application of qualitative methods to
institutional research.*

Summary Notes

*S. V. Martorana
Eileen Kuhns*

Definitions

Michael Quinn Patton provides the definitional framework
for this volume. He proposes that most researchers are professionally socialized to accept and use either the hypothetico-deductive
natural science paradigm or the holistic-inductive anthropological
paradigm, but not both. He compares the two paradigms in terms
of measurement, design, analysis, and basic purposes in terms of
prediction, or understanding of social phenomena.

Stressing that neither paradigm is intrinsically superior, he
recommends a new paradigm, a paradigm of choices, which "recognizes that different methods are appropriate for different situations." Furthermore, he notes that qualitative and quantitative
approaches can be combined in a mixed model, which he discusses
elsewhere with detailed examples (Patton, 1980).

Interpretive Evaluation

In his chapter exploring the contributions of anthropology
and sociology to qualitative research methods, Norman K. Denzin

E. Kuhns, S. V. Martorana (Eds.). *New Directions for Institutional Research: Qualitative
Methods for Institutional Research*, no. 34. San Francisco: Jossey-Bass, March 1982.

focuses on interpretive evaluation rather than on qualitative institutional studies per se. As he points out, interpretive evaluation demands a commitment "to enter actively the worlds of those studied so as to render those worlds understandable within an interpretive framework that is grounded in the behaviors, interactions, languages, meanings, symbolic forms, and emotions of those studied."

He distinguishes interpretive evaluation from evaluation research, and contrasts it with the positivistic quantitative paradigm. Research strategies for interpretive evaluation include participant observation; the life history of individuals, groups or organizations; case study construction; open-ended interviewing; and the collection of behavior specimens, "a fine-grained record of social interaction in natural social situations." Noting that these strategies are analytically inseparable, he calls them the fundamental tools of the qualitative researcher.

Denzin refers to his discussion of "traditional quantitative questions," such as reliability, validity, sampling, generalizability, causal adequacy, and causal analysis, in an earlier publication (Denzin, 1978) and proceeds to address three other interrelated questions, those of authenticity, thick description, and verisimilitude. Drawing on the work of Heidegger (1962), he illustrates the "circle of understanding" that underlies the evaluation process, which has at its center the investigator as participant observer. Finally, he explores the question of objectivity and the relation between knowledge and power from the viewpoint of the qualitative researcher.

A New Vocabulary and Grammar

Reducing the arbitrariness of description is a major objective of the chapter by F. Craig Johnson and R. C. Lacher on the contributions of mathematics to qualitative research methods. They are of the opinion that learning a new vocabulary and practicing indicated grammar rules will improve communication among researchers socialized according to different paradigms. It will also modify attitudes toward traditional research methods and clarify problems that have been insoluble. This chapter introduces a dozen terms for this new vocabulary, including *qualitative, dynamical systems, local maxima* and *minima, delay rule, Maxwell's rule, voting rule, steepest ascent, bifurcation, hysteresis, saddle point, cusp catastrophe,* and *vector field.* These terms, as well as others used to describe the grammar rules, such as *parameterized* and *coordinatized,* may not be familiar to the nonmathematician, but they are used in context by the authors to facilitate understanding. The postulates, assumptions, and hypotheses that form their qualitative model constitute the grammar rules.

Johnson and Lacher illustrate their approach through a decision-making model for admissions standards. In their example, the administration wants to please the various constituencies but is afraid of change; there is a range of options for an admissions policy; and opinion-gathering techniques are present that accurately discover the distribution of opinion relative to these options. Assuming that three stated postulates hold, the analysis proceeds to relate the altering of admissions standards to the opinion distribution.

The authors suggest that this approach provides a theoretical framework for all institutional research studies. Only summarized in their chapter, this possibility is explored further in a paper presented in 1981 at the European Association for Institutional Research Forum.

A Mixed Model

Research in political science has been dominated by the hypothetico-deductive natural science paradigm, according to Northrop and Kraemer, while public administration research has reflected the holistic-inductive anthropological paradigm. Of late, however, public administration also has been turning to quantitative methods, especially by moving away from case studies to probability samples.

Assuming that neither paradigm is intrinsically superior, a mixed model sets the advantages of each paradigm against the disadvantages of the other approach. Their four-year study of the management of computing in local government illustrates such a mixed model. After outlining Denzin's (1978) categories of triangulation, they describe their direct mixing of qualitative and quantitative methods in an approach termed *holistic triangulation.* Aspects of their study that mixed quantitative and qualitative methods included the combining of survey research, based on probability sampling of cities, with field observations; use of sampling theory to guide the choice of information-processing tasks to study; the random and purposeful sampling methods used for respondent selection, specifically tailored to each information-processing task; and the use of semistructured field-coded questionnaires along with self-administered questionnaires.

The authors also discuss benefits of the mixed model. Field collection of qualitative data permits the confirmation or rejection of conclusions reached on the basis of quantitative data. The combination of probability sampling with case study collection of data has the twin benefits of generalizability and in-depth understanding.

Events in Context

The professional outlook and training of historians predisposes them to examine events in their whole context, contends Mark H. Curtis in his chapter on the contributions of history to qualitative methodology. History is not what happened but what people do to acquire reliable knowledge about what happened and to translate that knowledge into an understanding of reality and their place in the world.

The historian is caught up in the process that he or she is trying to understand. Although there are pitfalls to avoid, the fact of this involvement does not make historical study invalid. The antidote to possible distortion, Curtis says, is the combination of disinterestedness and sensitivity to context. For the historian, context has two meanings. First, any thought or act is a part of the web of experience and indeed a function of it. Second, the past is part of the context of the present; that is, to comprehend what is requires us to understand what was.

The historian recognizes that each situation is unique, that it cannot be replicated to provide a control or comparison case. For qualitative research controls, he suggests comparing "what has come to be with what was" and "sophisticated contrast of differential development" in similar cases. To illustrate the latter approach, the author describes a project that evaluated the impact of the Institutional Grants Program of the National Endowment for the Humanities. As director of this national study, he addressed two major questions through historical research: how institutional grants had served national interests, and how institutional grants had met the needs of the colleges and universities that received them.

The concern with context and the recognition that each situation is unique are the basic contributions of history to qualitative methodology.

Impact of College on Students

With the chapter authored by Richard L. Alfred, the discussion moves from contributions of the various disciplines to qualitative methodology to applications of qualitative methodology at the institutional level. Alfred focuses on improving institutional decisions through qualitative research on students. He examines decisions that can and should be addressed through qualitative research, suggests data-collection strategies, and outlines the application of qualitative research data to decisions about students.

Alfred's work recognizes the press of diminishing institutional resources on the type of research on students that is currently emphasized. In this type of research, data collection tends to be quantitative, and the student is viewed as the generator of resources, not as the locus of research on educational development. Student flow data are necessary to respond to questions about the cost benefits of education, but they leave unanswered questions about the impact of college on students. "Informed decisions," he states, "require qualitative data" to identify desirable outcomes of college attendance, to develop programs and services that can improve these outcomes, and to relate the quality of outcomes to programs and services.

The author then describes an ideal holistic-inductive strategy for obtaining qualitative data about students, but he concludes that the costs in time and training render this ideal neither practical nor possible. In its place, he suggests a modified qualitative approach, with limited objectives, specific decision areas, and the identification of qualitative data that address the research objectives and decision targets. To elaborate this modified approach, he presents a model for research that comprises three stages of student interaction with the college environment: entry, intervening, and exit stages. The model includes a series of representative questions for each stage that helps to determine the focus of research for institutional and extrainstitutional decisions about students.

Pass-Fail Grading

Arthur Levine's chapter on qualitative research in academic decision making is almost entirely devoted to description of a campus visit arranged to collect information about a pass-fail grading system. This campus was chosen because its pass-fail system was held to be very successful. Having observed such systems on a number of other campuses, the author wanted to learn first-hand what accounted for the reported success of this one.

This visit lasted only two days, and while the design was a short-term type of qualitative research, it included the three principal kinds of qualitative data collection: in-depth interviews, document search, and observation. Prior to his visit, an institutional research effort at the college had included faculty and student surveys, both attitudinal and factual. Arriving at the college, Levine observed, interviewed, and searched documents, such as written evaluations of students' progress, minutes of faculty meetings, and student newspaper accounts. He interviewed the principals identified in his readings. This included the registrar, who was and remained an opponent of the pass-fail grading system. The list also included both commuting and resident students and opponents and proponents among the faculty.

His brief study uncovered a sharp divergence from the successful image that the pass-fail plan has enjoyed on the basis of survey data. In particular, his study unearthed several rather serious unintended outcomes of the plan. For example, several graduate departments had decided not to admit undergraduates whose transcripts showed more than a certain percentage of pass-fail courses. As Levine notes, information from such a study is not only valueable for decision making but also for identifying decisions that will have to be made; that is, such qualitative research becomes an early-warning system for an institution's decision makers. He describes this short-term kind of qualitative study as "cheap, easy, and fast." Comprehensive qualitative measurement, design, and analysis can be expensive, difficult, and time-consuming, as Richard Alfred noted in the preceding chapter.

Action Meaning and Act Meaning

Michael Tierney focuses on the applicability of qualitative methods in management decisions. As introduction to the chapter he gives a brief historical background of the origins of the qualitative-quantative controversy, noting that the underlying question concerns the kinds of understanding that are possible in the social sciences. One branch of this approach to understanding originated in Max Weber's ideal type; this line of research into action meaning has culminated in quantitative models. The second branch emerged from the qualitative methods required for understanding unique events, for understanding act meaning from the viewpoint of those involved. The two branches are complementary types of understanding in the social sciences. Action meaning research addresses the meaning of the act to social scientists; that is, the meaning of behavior in terms of theory. Act meaning designs explore what the event signifies to the actor, whose perspective is embedded in that person's values, norms, and experiences.

Next, Tierney concentrates on research methods appropriate to investigation of act meaning for principals involved in management decisions at colleges and universities. He regards finance decisions as the subset of management decisions concerned with who will share in paying for institutional programs and activities.

Tierney focuses on the annual budget cycle to illustrate the use of qualitative research methods to explore act meaning. An accompanying flow chart depicts the budget trade-off decisions which must be made. This contrasts with the more usual flow chart, which shows when budget actions are to occur during the cycle. He suggests that the sequence of these trade-off decisions is related to the type of institution in which these decisions are made. The complex set of trade-offs involves ranking the values held by the principal actors in the budget process. The qualitative study of what the decision trade-offs mean to participants reveals these values; in this example, the values are concerned with fiscal solvency, academic program quality, and faculty morale. Awareness of these value priorities in turn alerts senior administrators about possible conflict or consensus among key decision makers.

Strengthening Educational Practice

Understanding and strengthening educational practice through the use of a mixed model involving both qualitative and quantitative research is the focus of the chapter by Jerry Gaff. Implicit is his message that, for the problems of the sixties, the seventies, and now the eighties, faculty need systematic analysis to help them to help themselves. Explicit is his message that faculty are socialized through background and past experience about the appropriate forms of educational practice, but their views can be naive, simplistic, or wrong. Needed, says Gaff, is research that encourages faculty to conceptualize their own views, subject them to critical analysis, test them in practice, and consider alternatives that can help them to achieve their own purposes. Researchers and faculty need one another. Faculty need the perspectives and knowledge available through educational research; researchers need to have their findings utilized in actual practice.

Gaff has had the opportunity to conduct comprehensive research on three distinct approaches to improvement of undergraduate education: the cluster college in the sixties, faculty development in the seventies, and curriculum reform in the current decade. In each case, he studied isolated experiments, using essentially what Mark Curtis called the sophisticated contrast of differential development in similar cases. Each project used a mixed model involving both quantitative and qualitative measurement and design. An important purpose of each study was to provide postsecondary education faculty with perspectives and knowledge about educational practice designed to improve undergraduate education. From these complex research efforts, Gaff has developed a set of principles to guide the use of such a mixed model and to facilitate utilization of its findings. He states that research in higher education would be more effective if more attention was paid to the qualitative paradigm, but he concludes that an imbalance in the direction of either paradigm would be counterproductive.

The Measurement of Quality

The definition and measurement of quality itself is an issue that institutional researchers can address through the use of qualitative methodology. George Bonham opens his discussion with questions about the indices of quality at the macro level. He notes that professional educators and the general public, including their elected representatives, do not necessarily agree on measures of quality in education. Moving into the academic setting, he lists some of the sacred cows by which institutions measure themselves qualitatively, reminding us that even if these measures are maximized, none of them guarantees a quality education.

He attributes the surge of interest in measuring quality and in acting on that measurement to money or the lack thereof and to the lowering of standards "brought about by wider inclusion of new learners from intellectually less-favored backgrounds." When value added is considered, however, the best potential for educational improvement may lie near the bottom of the bell curve, which may confound the measurement of academic quality.

Acknowledging the decline of quality in American education, he says, should be distinguished from defining and measuring that quality. Especially if the approach is quantitative, the issues may be obscured, since splendid learning environments can be unassuming in their measurable structure. In his former role as editor-in-chief of *Change* magazine, Bonham encouraged financial analyses of institutional health and reputational ratings of academic institutions. The second study evolved from his concern with academic quality.

The next question was that of quality at the micro level; that is, the relation of the institution's reputation to the educational development of individual students. Assessing the educational quality of an institution on the basis of either inputs or outputs is a risky endeavor, with the question of value added emerging as a central problem. Bonham puts emphasis on the concept of value added. For measuring value added, the procedures of qualitative methodology described by other authors in this volume may well be the most promising.

A Note on "Additional Resources"

Because the first five chapters focus on qualitative methodology in the various disciplines and are replete with references that themselves constitute additional resources, only a few more resources are listed here, together with the references cited in this summary chapter.

Additional Resources

Carney, T. F. *Content Analysis: A Technique for Systematic Inference from Communications.* Winnipeg: University of Manitoba Press, 1972.

Edwards, W., Guttentag, M., and Snapper, K. "A Decision-Theoretic Approach to Evaluation Research." In E. L. Struening and M. Guttentag (Eds.), *Handbook of Evaluation Research.* Vol. 1. Beverly Hills, Calif.: Sage, 1975.

Denzin, N. K. *The Research Act.* (2nd ed.) New York: McGraw-Hill, 1978.

Fehrenbacher, H. L., Owens, T. R., and Haenn, J. F. *The Use of Student Case Study Methodology in Program Evaluation.* Research Evaluation Development Paper Series, No. 10. Portland, Ore.: Northwest Regional Educational Laboratory, 1976.

Heidegger, M. *Being and Time.* New York: Harper, 1962.

Johnson, F. C., and Lacher, R. C. "Contributions of Nonlinear Dynamical Systems to Decision Making." Paper presented at the European Association for Institutional Research Forum, Louvain la-Nouve, Belgium, 1981. Available through the authors at Florida State University.

Patton, M. Q. *Qualitative Evaluation Methods.* Beverly Hills, Calif.: Sage, 1980.

"Qualitative Research: A Summary of the Concepts Involved." *Journal of the Market Research Society,* 1979, *21* (2), 107–124.

Rist, R. C. "Blitzkrieg Ethnography: On the Transformation of a Method into a Movement." *Educational Researcher,* 1980, *9* (2), 8–10.

Scriven, M. "Pros and Cons About Goal-Free Evaluation." *Evaluation Comment,* 1972, *3,* 1–7.

Sechrest, L. (Ed.). *New Directions for Methodology of Social and Behavioral Science: Unobtrusive Measurement Today,* no. 1. San Francisco: Jossey-Bass, 1979.

Stake, R. E. "The Case Study Method in a Social Inquiry." *Educational Researcher,* 1978, 7 (2), 5–8.

S. V. Martorana is a professor in the College of Education and a research associate in the Center for the Study of Higher Education, Pennsylvania State University.

Eileen Kuhns is an associate professor and coordinator of the Education Administration Program, Catholic University of America. They are codirectors of a FIPSE-funded project designed to institutionalize an interorganizational, interstate program of regionwide planning for postsecondary education.

Index